CRISSIE CAUGHLIN *PIONEER*

CRISSIE CAUGHLIN
~ Pioneer ~

By

Shiela Lonie

To Joan Gassiot

Enjoy
Shiela Lonie

Black Rock Press
2004

Copyright © 2004 by Shiela Lonie
All rights reserved.
This book, or parts thereof, may not be reproduced in any form
without written permission, except in the case of brief
quotations embodied in critical articles and reviews.
For information, please address the publisher.

ISBN 1-891033-26-3

The Black Rock Press
University Library/322
University of Nevada, Reno
Reno, NV 89557-0044

www.library.unr.edu/blackrock

To my perfect children—Stacie, Richard, and Syrene—my grandchildren, and to all the future generations to come.

CONTENTS

	Preface	xi
	Acknowledgements	xiii
1	Crissies Grandparents, Benjamin and Hannah Andrew	1
2	Crissie's Parents, George and Bettie	15
3	Crissie's Aunts and Uncles	37
4	Crissie	53
5	Crissie Faces Death and Divorce	67
6	Crissie's Marriage and Family	79
7	Crissie Caughlin's Children	101
8	Crissie's Ranch, The Andrews/Caughlin Ranch	121
9	Reno Ranch Celebrities	141
10	Crissie's Battle for Water Rights	151
11	Caughlin Ranch Development	159
12	Crissie's Final Goodbye	167

Appendix

Crissie's Library	181
Chapter Notes	187
Bibliography	193
Index	195
The Author	207

ACKNOWLEDGEMENTS

So many people have helped me in making Grandma Crissie's story into a book. At a large fundraiser at Lake Tahoe in the fall of 1997, I met Wayne Melton and told him my dream of writing my book. He was so supportive and encouraging that the seed was planted. I showed the many boxes of letters, pictures, and rare artifacts to Gregor Peterson, a neighbor and publisher. He was amazed at the wealth of history my grandmother had kept from over a 150-year period. He told me Bob Blesse, head of Special Collections at the University of Nevada, Reno was the person to contact.

The first step was bringing order to the collection and placing it in a safe location for use by historians, scholars, and students for generations to come. Fred Holabird appraised Crissie's collection. Susan Searcy, who is now at the Nevada State Archives, saw the beginning and the ending of this project. She helped with the original appraisal and organized Crissie's collection of letters and photographs from the 1850s through 1955 and ledgers that document the Caughlin Ranch history for donation to the UNR Special Collections Department in the Getchell Library. Most photographs have names and dates written on them. Most letters are in their original envelopes with dates and postmarks. Susan also helped edit the final manuscript for this book.

At Special Collections, Bob Blesse deserves special thanks for recognizing the value of Crissie's collection and, as head of the Black Rock Press, for designing and publishing Crissie's book. Archivist Kathy Totton took special care in organizing the hundreds of photographs. Fred Cornelius took excellent photographs of Crissie's treasures that remain as keepsakes in my family.

Three dressed and other clothing items were donated to the Marjorie Russell Clothing and Textile Research Center of the Nevada Division of Museums and History in Carson City, Nevada. I enjoyed learning more about the dresses from Curator Jan Loverin.

My thanks goes to Alma (Schiappacasse) Westegard for her first-hand remembrances of my grandmother and to her niece Prilla Fordham for making the arrangements for the oral history interview with Alma.

Once again, I want to thank Bob Blesse for highly recommending Victoria Ford to help me throughout this project as my editor, and she assisted with research. We have turned into soul mates and newest best friends. We share the same birthday (November 1). I shall always be most grateful for her help.

Nearly all of the letters were transcribed exactly as written and then edited for grammar and spelling to make them easier to read.

I am proud to thank another star in my galaxy, Whitney Williamson, my granddaughter and creative art director for the Crocker & Flanagan advertising agency in Sacramento. I have enjoyed working with each person who helped me.m

Shiela Lonie

PREFACE

My grandmother, Crissie Caughlin, always had a twinkle in her eyes and a quiet mystique. Even as a small child, I knew she possessed secrets. The old ranch house with its four large bedrooms and closets upstairs held wondrous treasures. Seven old trunks were filled with even more mysteries. In the hall at the top of the stairs was a small pump organ, which we were allowed to play when we were older, and a cabinet filled with very old books, lots of music and children's books.

After my father's unexpected, early death at 55, my mother and I were living at the ranch house with Grandma Crissie (as everyone called her). She brought a long box filled with letters to the kitchen table. A faded blue ribbon tied the letters together. The stamps were very old and the addresses were of the style long before zip codes. They were addressed to Mrs. Bettie Andrews, Reno, Nevada; Mrs. Wm. Caughlin, 215 South Verdi Road (now Mayberry Drive), Reno; George Washington Andrews, Washoe City, Nevada. When Grandma Crissie started to read these letters, I was transported back in time and history to the Civil War. I followed the many journeys of all our family members, who came from far eastern states to Nevada.

As an adult, my children were still very young when we moved to Piedmont, California in 1969. Being a newcomer, I was invited to join a book club. Mrs. Truman, a member, was a reviewer who made stories come alive. When I told her about the old letters, she lit up and said, "You must write a book about your family."

The seed was sewn. As the years passed, some family members told me not to put this or that story into the book. I said nothing, but in order to tell the true stories, I decided to wait until the older generation was gone. After Grandma Crissie died, we found an unbelievable collection of letters, documents, photographs, jewelry, and dresses dating back to 1850. After Aunt Betsy died, the last of Crissie's children, we discovered even more treasures; she never threw anything away.

Through the years, Crissie had given me many heirlooms—jewelry and dishes, Sandy Bowers's canister, and a marble-top table that once belonged to Governor John Sparks. In my first home, I put her marble-top table in my front hall where I kept her silver and crystal pickle dish filled with fresh-cut spring flowers. She laughed with delight when she saw it, because she knew I loved her antiques and would cherish them always.

At last, the time has come for telling Crissie's story. Crissie and her children are gone, my children are grown with families of their own, and I am widowed for the second time. Now, I have opened all the trunks and boxes of old letters, looked at Reno and Nevada history, and studied my family's contributions. Now the time has come to tell these untold stories.

Shiela Lonie
2004

CHAPTER ONE
Crissie's Grandparents
Benjamin and Hannah Andrew

My grandmother Christine Harriet Andrews Caughlin was a first generation native Nevadan, daughter of one of Reno's earliest ranchers, a university graduate, mother of four, ranch owner and operator, and a prominent member in several Reno women's organizations. Today, nearly every Renoite knows the location of the Caughlin Ranch development in prestigious southwest Reno. Some have walked by the Truckee River at Crissie Caughlin Park or strolled through the park donated by Crissie's daughter, Betsy Caughlin Donnelly, at the corner of Mayberry Drive and McCarran Boulevard. A few realize that the white, two-story house nearby is the Caughlin ranch house. Rarely do you meet anyone who knows that Horseman's Park off Skyline Boulevard and the home of the Carmelite nuns are part of the legacy Crissie left to Reno.

Crissie's story actually began back east where her parents were born. Her father, George Washington Andrew, came west from New Hampshire and her mother, Bettie Hughes, came from Maine. George and Bettie's story is filled with drama, adventure, love, commitment, joy, and heartbreak—one of many such stories that has survived the years since the great westward migration of the mid-1800s.

From her parents, Crissie inherited the many traits needed to operate a ranch near Reno—determination, resilience, hard work, and steadfast devotion to her family and the land. Against all odds, this amazing woman's story is preserved in letters dating back to the Civil War, all carefully passed down through four generations to me. Saved also were photographs, and many were methodically named and dated. Thus, Crissie's legacy goes beyond the Caughlin Ranch in Reno. It includes her family's story of emigrating to the West and pioneering in Nevada.

THE ANDREW FAMILY

Gathering information on ancestors who lived in the 1700s and 1800s was like discovering missing pieces to a long-lost puzzle.

Thank goodness my Great Grandfather George's sister Martha was a family historian. She faithfully recorded the Andrew's history for annual reunions and passed it along to Crissie through their lively correspondence.

George Washington Andrew was born and raised in New Hampshire.[1] George's grandparents, Samuel Andrew and Sarah Peaslee Andrew, were among the first settlers of Sutton, New Hampshire.

> Sarah Peaslee, b. Oct. 30, 1771 married July 4, 1791 [Independence Day] to Samuel Andrew, b. Jan. 16, 1770 and died March 1, 1837. Sarah (Sally) was the first female child born in Sutton that lived to maturity. Her father built the first house, kept the first tavern in the town, which was first named Perrystown. This was the south village. The church there is on the site selected by a town committee of which her father was one. The tavern was built on the main street and may be seen still with its front piazza facing west, its small windows having the old "4x9" panes. Sally Peaslee Andrew was my grandmother and here was her playground in childhood and the place where buzzed her spinning wheel and loom; until, at the age of 20, she and my grandfather were married.

Martha's letter listed ten children born to Samuel and Sally between 1792 and 1810, four daughters and six sons. George's father, Benjamin Andrew, was the youngest.

Benjamin Randall Andrew
b. June 29, 1810, d. November 21, 1875

A native of Sutton, the son of Samuel and Sally (Peaslee) Andrew, Benjamin settled in New London soon after reaching manhood, and in a residence of more than forty years proved himself worthy of the respect of his fellow-townsmen. His wife was Hannah Blanchard, daughter of Greene and Molly (Page) French, and they resided on the French homestead. Benjamin died November 21, 1875 and Hannah died two days later on November 23, 1875. They were buried together, the funeral being held at the church. Children were George Washington, born February 10, 1834, a resident of Clark's Station, Nevada;[2] Martha Jane, born May 23, 1841; and Mary Emeline French, born February 19, 1845.[3]

On Hannah's side, the French family was also well known and highly respected among early New Hampshire settlers. Hannah and Benjamin were each the youngest children in their families.

Benjamin Randall Andrew, b. June 29, 1810, d. Nov. 21, 1875, Crissie's paternal grandfather

Hannah Blanchard French was the youngest daughter of Greene French, and became a successful teacher. She married Benj. R. [Benjamin Randall] Andrew of North Sutton and lived at the old [French family] homestead where they reared three children: George Washington, so named by his patriotic grandfather Greene French; Martha Jane; and Mary Emeline French, so named for the grandmother who had pronounced her "too pretty to live" – yet, she *did* live and became the pet of the family and of the neighbors. George W. was a teacher in the common schools of Orange, Wilmot and New London. He was in business in Boston and afterward taught school in Halifax.

Hannah's first-born child and only son George was the apple of her eye. In later years, his younger sisters remembered a big brother who "had a peculiar disposition" and was mischievous, often pulling pigtails and playing pranks.

New London, N.H.
February 17, 1863

Dear George,
....You remember, that [pond] is where you and Willard Davis, along with other scrapes, produced such a conflagration. Mother told me about it, and by the way, weren't you in your young days full of the very "old Boy?" to use a very unladylike expression. I have a faint recollection of your coming home very late nights and rising very late the next *afternoon*.
        Sister Mary

June 21, 1915

Dear Crissie,
 Again I breathe the air of Antrim—the namesake of the wonderful County of Ireland from which your ancestors fled from English tyranny and from which they immigrated to America.
 Orange was the town where your father taught his first school before he was 21. He was so homesick that he came home on foot one time, Friday night through a hard snowstorm. There he learned about working in the steam mill. I was a little girl but remember just how he looked.
        Aunt Martha[4]

In the 1850s, young George traveled west in search of his fortune along with thousands of other young men. Martha's letters told the story of George's trip by sea.

Hannah Buchanan French Andrew, b. Sept. 23, 1809, d. Nov. 23, 1875 Crissie's paternal grandmother

Benjamin Randall Andrew,
Crissie's Paternal Grandfather

Antrim, N.H.
October 25, 1915
(Part of a letter to Crissie's daughter Syrene)

…. I was not as old as you when George decided to go. He was the only son and, of course, the main dependence of father and mother. But he was "of age" and not obliged to stay. When he left, I saw the tears in his eyes, and I know he began to think what a break he was making of the family ties.

My mother looked every day for his return but it was "hoping against hope," for she was not to see him again on earth. When his letters came she cried. He told how sick he was on the steamer out from New York and of his crossing the isthmus, for he went by Panama, across to Aspinwall, and taking a steamer from there to San Francisco.

Then he began work in the Redwoods. At the sawmill of [William] Hughes [Bettie's brother William], he met… Bettie and they were married. But it was a long time before he wrote about it—and it so happened that another George Andrews was married to Mary Breslin—so the paper he sent us stated, and we thought for a long time that his wife's name was Mary.

Your loving
Aunt Martha

Only one letter from George's father has survived the past 140 years, along with a small handful of messages from his mother, but I know that for the rest of their lives, George's parents hoped to see their son again. These few letters speak volumes about how so many families must have felt when their children ventured to the West, never to return. Daily chores were harder for lack of a son's strong hands and fears for care in their old age increased without a son to care for them. In addition, Hannah and Benjamin's letters offer a glimpse into 1860s New Hampshire—the hard work, the crops, the meals, and the moral values that guided their lives. The world George entered in the West stood in stark contrast to the more civilized life he left behind in the East.

New London, 1860

Dear George,

I have delayed writing until now for the reason that I have not had any time, as I have not had anyone to help me this season. I hope that is not your excuse. If I could write as easy as you can, I would write oftener. Your mother is wondering why you don't write oftener. I hope you will write soon if you are not coming home. We are hoping that you may be at home soon, although I do not dare to advise you to come, as you must know better than myself. The prospect here is as good as it ever was and perhaps better.... If you should conclude to come home, you will find a plenty of apples and cider…, raised 100 and 50 bushels of ears of corn, rye, oats, and India wheat a plenty, and your colt is fat and slick and well broke.[5]

                              Benjamin Andrew

November 16, 1860
Ever Dear Son,

As your father has written to you, I feel it my duty to write also, but with a faint idea of this reaching you or your abode. I have looked and looked, again and again, for you or a letter. I have dreamed many times of your being at home with us, but nothing, but now and then a paper or magazine for [which] we feel highly gratified. I am very tired tonight so you must excuse me if I don't write but little.

You withhold writing for some reason; I know not what. Not one letter have we had from you.... Whether you wrote or have forgotten your friends at home is to me mysterious. I would tell you of good health did I enjoy it, but no. I feel I can never more have good health and spirits. I long to soar above these earthly trials sometimes. But, oh, how unfit to bear so many different problems, if among them I must part with my only son to stay in this distant country. I deserve to be reunited, but I sometimes feel that I may die of old age, uncared for.... I think how happy I must be if things were different, but of everything let us learn to be content. I must be done for the clock strikes eleven....

Your father carried seven bushels of India wheat to mill today. [We have] a plenty of hominy... and other good things. I guess we shall live well this winter.

George, my moral to you must be short... almost midnight. You are not yet too old to listen to me. Be sure to live an honest man. Remember a peaceful conscience in old age is the best heritage, but no matter what fools may say, be honorable in your tending with all your fellows. Don't let it be said California has lost one scaly boy when you have left, but rather let all mourn at your leaving. Please roll up your pile of clothes and come home even. I guess all are anxiously waiting your return.

                          From your mother,
                          Hannah Andrew
                          Our respects to your wife.[6]

Hannah Buchanan French Andrew, b. Sept. 23, 1809, d. Nov. 23, 1875, Crissie's paternal grandmother

New London, New Hampshire, the town where Crissie's father George Washington Andrew was born

> New London, N.H.
> May 26, 1861[7]
> Sunday 6 ½ o'clock
>
> Ever Dear Son,
> I was truly glad to receive yesterday your letter. I feel now you have done your duty. You have done well, once and again. I guess you are coming into your right mind. You seem to say something about coming home. I think there will be no risk in your coming [at] any time on account of your health, if you have not had ague. Your constitution is so strong I think you might come any time, except in the hottest weather when yellow fever rages in the hot climates. If you can get home, even if it is cold, we will keep you in blankets till warm weather. I think you had better get ready to come home as fast as you can. They complain about traveling in the western states, Iowa and Illinois and thereabouts.... Our deacon S. Stephen died of cancer last week. His wife is very low, must soon follow. We think Uncle Samuel Faler is but just alive. So you see we are passing away, one after another....
>
> From your mother,
> H.R.J. Andrews

New London
May 29, 1863

Ever Dear Son,
   ...We are calling ourselves in tolerable good health. How long I can say so is uncertain. Continued labor seems to wear

upon my feeble constitution so much that I feel sometimes about ready to say, I must continue [to find] some way to rest or my work is done surely. The summer work looks like a mountain before me – a cow to milk, butter to make, and so on.

George, I can hardly feel reconciled to have you away. I feel me one [step] nearer ruin as a family, [because we have] so much need of somebody to keep things right. Your father seems to care but little how things go much of the time. He says but little to me about anything, day or night, so you see I'm one of the poorest of widows. He won't even go to meeting [church service] with me. For a few winters past, I have not been able to go in cold weather. But now [that] it is warm, I should like to go. But he seems more like it makes [no difference to] him, anything, unless somebody comes in. If you were here, you might cheer him, perhaps, or save him from that ruinous path he seems too much inclined to walk. If you do not intend to come home, you ought to write and tell us.

I don't see why you won't come home…. I tell you, I feel about ready to sink under the weight of so many disappointments… but must close, writing to our far distant boy. I hope you will write soon and let us know how you are. They say you are married, but I don't credit such report until I hear from you. If it is so, be kind to your wife ever. Never deceive.

<blockquote>
This from your
mother
Hannah B.F. Andrews
</blockquote>

P.S. Your last letter was August 1862.

Andrew family home, New London, New Hampshire, July 1958

[Addressed to Silver Mountain, California, July 8, 1865.]
New London, N.H.
May 1865

Dear Friends,

We received a newspaper last Friday with a few words of information from you, the first we have seen for one year. We have written many letters but have had no answer to one of them…. We have been on the watch almost daily ever since [for] your arrival. I hope you will make a strong effort to write or come immediately home. Here is a plenty of work and good pay or pleasure riding on the trotting course or chatting with the boys and girls of school. Here, too, is your Uncle Simeon living north of us at present; and Mary, our school teacher of district school, wishing most awful George would come home.

What is the use to put up any inducement? Your will is just as strong as ever and you will do as you please, though shall I write in an acceptable manner?

Your cousin Byron Andrews, who has faithfully endured the [Civil] war will soon, we hope, meet his much loved friends again. I must witness their greeting, but what think you would be my feelings on meeting my *only son,* so much cared for in days gone by and even now causes so much anxiety in a Mother's heart, once full of expectation of her only son to cheer the days of her old age....

Your father is about as you left him – young, handsome, witty, talks much of going to California but will wait, I guess, till you come home. He will spend his best days in idle wishes instead of enjoying solid comforts. You may suppose me about as smart as any of the rest, as I do about all the work inside, but many changes have taken place in town since you left. Now, won't you muster courage to write to your friends at home?

From your mother,
H.B. Andrews

Andrew family home, New London, New Hampshire, July 1958

[undated]
Ever Dear Son,

I gladly embrace the opportunity of conversing with you even in this broken manner.... Your father says he should like to have you come home when you get ready and carry on the farm. He does seem tired of work. Seems healthy but doesn't want to work so hard. He does most of the milking. I made the first cheese yesterday -- have made some butter.... Supper over. We [had] wheat bread, butter, fried cakes and cherry sauce, and tea composed our supper.... Helen Andrews is coming to school this fall. Takes so much, but I must let the girls [sisters Martha and Mary] go again this fall. I guess they will go as long as I live, so they will have some learning, if nothing more.... How soon when you will start for home? Don't let the Indians trouble you. Use them well. And George, be sure to take care of your health. Go to church often as possible. Strive to be a Christian that your life may be happy and death a welcome friend. I thank you very much for your kindness in sending papers.

Yours affectionately,
Hannah B. Andrews

THE CIVIL WAR

George's mother mentioned relatives who fought in the Civil War. His two younger sisters, Martha and Mary, expressed strong patriotic feelings about the war, and listed details of their neighbors and friends, who left home to fight for the North.

New London, N.H.
May 26, 1861

My Dear Only Brother;
How gladly did we receive a letter from you last evening! Also three papers.
...the harvest may be abundant, for I think there will be need of an abundance of provisions this year on account of the war. If war is openly declared, it will be a long and bloody one. I think Lincoln will find that the last rail that he has split will be a rough and tough one. I guess he will wish he had let the tree remain standing. The Republican party (how utterly unworthy the name of Republican!) which, but a few years ago, favored the plan of disunion, who said "let the union slide," and a number of which said in the *N.Y. Tribune*, "All hail, disunion, etc." that party will soon see, if they are not *blind*, that their principles do not work for their good. *Now* they say the Union must be preserved....

Jack Sargent was appointed recruiting officer for this portion of the county, and all those that enlisted from a part of the towns around here applied to him. Reuben Porter of Sutton, Wingate Rowe of Wilmot Flat were two that went. Rowe had quite an office appointed to him. Jack Sargent is captain of the Keene Company. They encamped at Concord on the Fairground. Yesterday they expected to start for some station near the seat of war. That was the first regiment. The second is at Portsmouth expecting to go if called for. Alfred Eaton of Bradford or Newbury, or where you taught school, is in that regiment. His brother John Eaton is here at school. He rooms in Aunt Mary's with a young man by the name of Gage who has a brother in the southern Army. Jack Sargent, before he went to Concord, took a ride to Vermont with Oliver Russell. They returned Monday afternoon. They passed here with a lady, whom we afterwards found to be Jack's *wife*.

Yesterday, May 25, they (the inhabitants of the town) met and voted that there should be appropriated to the use of those who had enlisted from this town, two hundred dollars. Jack Sargent, captain of the McCutchins's Guards, a military company formed here; Lieut. Joseph Clough, Hugh Clough's son; a fellow by the name of McFarland, who came here to

Martha Andrew Byers, Crissie's aunt and the Andrew's family historian

school, enlisted here, and the town adopted him: and another named Quimby were all that went from New London. Mother is very much concerned for fear you will join the army. It does not seem to me that California will send any troops. But if they do, I suppose you will not join them, but mother thinks you would be very likely to. I think if I were a boy I should enlist, and if it were necessary to shed my blood for the support of my country, for the preservation of the Union, I would willingly do so. Civil war is not without its horrors, but the country is a dear one. It was bought by the blood of our forefathers and it must be sustained, if it costs more lifeblood.

Your affectionate
Sister, Martha Jane

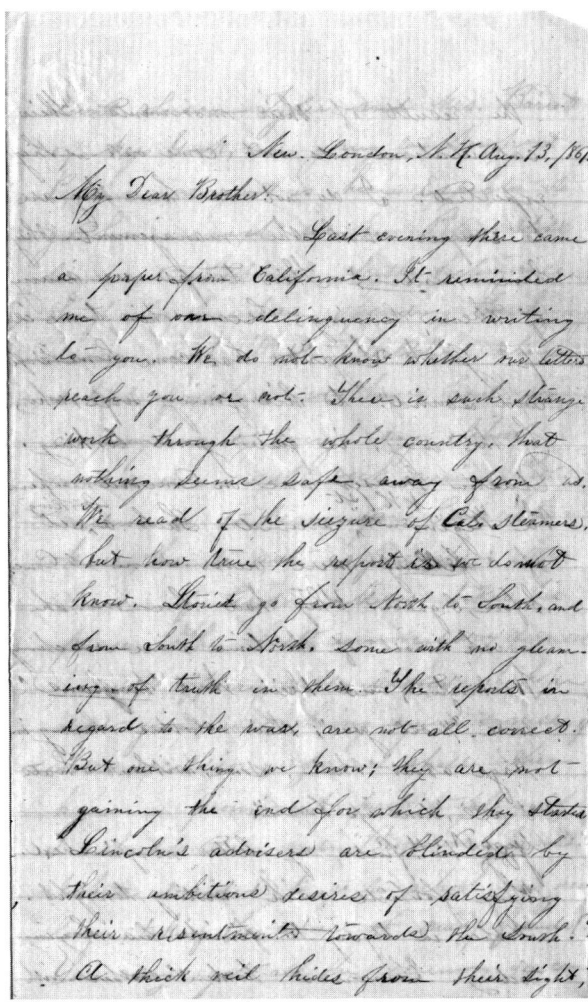

Letter from Martha to George,
August 13, 1861

*New London,
N.H. Aug. 13, 1861*

My Dear Brother

Last evening there came a paper from California…. We read of the seizure of California steamers, but how true the report is we do not know. Stories go from North to South and from South to North, some with no gleaming of truth in them. The reports in regard to the war are not all correct. But one thing we know; they are not gaining the end for which they started. Lincoln's advisers are blinded by their ambitious desires of satisfying their resentments towards the South. A thick veil hides from their sight the results of their movements. Their calculations do not come out as they expected. I do not see how they are to conquer with the managements they have made. Their troops are many of them leaving, because their time is up.

Jack Sargent has come home safe and sound to his young wife, who, by the way, is quite good looking. Austin Misser was in Concord when the Regiment (N.H. 1st) arrived; such a looking set of fellows were never seen at Concord before, I guess. They had been on the march most of the time since reaching Washington, and their thick "brogans" were "most gone;" their clothes hung in rags about them, some without hats and all "done up brown."

Your Sister
Martha

New London,
N.H. Oct. 13, 1861

My Dear Brother;
    We have been waiting – waiting for a letter from you. No word comes. We have written to you twice, I think, since we received your last. We sometimes hear war news from the West. California sends her aid to preserve the union. I was about to say the glorious union – but 'tis now no longer glorious – for the affinity seems broke off by a strange element and a part is alienated. The South has separated and instead of "E Pluribus Unum" we are plurinum ex un. It is a sad thing for such a war to happen to this once happy people – but it may be a just judgment for so many dissensions of party as we have had. Party strife is not yet crushed – nor ever will it be. Union, peaceable union, will never be ours. Many are leaving their homes "to fight for the Stars and Stripes" but I fear it will be in vain. Jack Sargent returned and his company. Reuben Porter came back at the same time. Joseph Clough has gone again as Captain of some company. Ed Stinson has enlisted. Jerome Porter has gone in a company of "Sharp Shooters." Mr. McFarland, who left school last spring and went with Jack, came back with his $50 given him by this town and his wages at war and, with his wife, is now attending school. He is the janitor of the Academy. Things do not seem to be *much* changed here on account of the war. *Some* articles are getting higher. "They can't afford to buy lemons. They cost $8 a box and they can't afford it."
    Father says, "This war is a disgraceful one, the greatest calamity that ever happened to any nation." He has forgotten how to write and you must not expect any more letters from him, but I think he doesn't want to put his glasses on.
                              Martha

French family reunion 1905

New London, N.H.
August 28th, 1862

My dear Brother:
    This afternoon we received your letter dated August 1st. Our hearts were glad. I assure you Mother *danced,* fairly, and we eagerly grasped the ideas. How much better it made us feel.... Yesterday morning 46 of our townsmen started for the war.... Many were the moistened eyes, the aching hearts, choking voices as they said good-bye. Ah! I knew what it was to part with a brother, but I could not sympathize with those who sent their brothers to sustain so noble a cause as these 46 men have gone forth to do. I thought I should have

George's excellent penmanship and artistic drawings revealed he had talents beyond hauling lumber

felt better if I had a brother to send, or better still, had I been a boy to join their ranks, to accompany them to the field of strife, to share with them the soldier's noble death or glorious victory. It may, and perhaps it does, seem strange that I, a feeble selfish female, should make such a speech as this. But where is the *patriotism* of her who says to Father, Brother, or Son, "You must not go?" Low in the dust lies our country's glorious flag, and who but our brave northern men can raise it again—drenched as it is in blood drawn by a brother from a brother's veins! Let the tears of America's daughters moisten the soil our Pilgrim Fathers gained for them. Yes, and even spill *their* blood if needs be - to save the tottering government. Father thinks of going to war....

    Sister Mary[8]

New London, N.H.
February 17, 1863 and
March 18, 1863

....I think I never knew people so interested in election before this year. The Republicans had secret meetings, introduced a third party.... It is hardly pardonable for a Democrat to speak his opinion. Father has been ordered to stop his "secession talk" a number of times, and once was told by Hon. Joseph Phillips to "leave the shop or we'll put you out." But Father maintained his ground and remained still speaking the same...

    [letter from Mary and Martha]

Crab Orchard, Kentucky
April 12, 1864

My Dear Brother,
I have at last arrived in Kentucky. I have wanted to go south for so long a time.... I am to begin a small school tomorrow. I act as governess in a family. I shall have probably about a dozen or less scholars. The lady gives me $25 per month, boards me, and does my washing....

The papers say that a rebel raid is expected in the interior of this state. If so, they will pass directly through this place. They have been here once, but they will not harm me. I shall not be afraid....

Goodbye this time, more soon,
Sister Martha

George's parents remained in New Hampshire, and like so many others who went West, George never returned to New Hampshire nor saw his parents again. He did see his sister Martha, when she visited him in Reno at Thanksgiving of 1874 or 1875. At that time, she lived in Elko, Nevada, where her husband served as a minister.

THE HUGHES FAMILY

Crissie's mother Bettie Hughes came from a background that was very different from George Andrew's upbringing. Even though both were raised in Christian communities and both knew hard work, Bettie's early life held more hardship than George's. Bettie's mother died when she was just 6 years old, and her father died when she was 13. While George was the "ever dear son," Bettie was orphaned and had to make her own way in the world by boarding out and working for other families. George's mother was a teacher and made sure her children received an excellent education. No record of Bettie's education remains, although we do know Bettie and her sister Jane had to work for their room and board.

These were the two very different young adults, George and Bettie, who gathered their courage and traveled across the continent to the raw, new territory outside the borders of the United States. Thus began Crissie's pioneer family.

∽ CHAPTER TWO ∽
Crissie's Parents
George and Bettie

GEORGE WASHINGTON ANDREWS of New Hampshire and Bettie Hughes of Maine, both born in 1834, were in their twenties when they traveled to California searching for a pot of gold, a better climate, and a new life. When Bettie first arrived from the East, she stayed at the home of her brother William and his wife Harriet at Pescadero, California, where William owned and operated a lumber mill. George was his employee.

COURTSHIP

George and Bettie had little time for a formal courtship. In 1862, an early spring flood damaged William's mill so badly that he packed up his wife Harriet, his sister Bettie and all their belongings and traveled to one of Nevada's newest boomtowns, Aurora. The move was made in wagons pulled by oxen over rough, narrow roads. One friend back east expressed concern for Bettie's safety.

Rochester
March 12th, 1862

Friend Bettie,
   ...received your letter last week and was very glad to hear from you.... I was very sorry to hear of your troubles in California. I had seen an account of the flood but did not think that it was near your place. I wish you had never gone there at all. I think you would have done better to have stayed here. Do not go away up over those mountains. I beg of you; if there is any possible way for you to get back to New York, do come....
                               Yours in haste,
                               Mary E. Pinkham

However, Bettie did go "up over those mountains" just days after she and George met. Her letters to George, who stayed behind in California, contained vivid descriptions of the hardships as they traveled treacherous mountain roads. They were met by a complete lack of amenities when they arrived at their destination. In fact, these letters became the entire courtship between George and

Bettie. Etiquette of the day gave way to economic necessity, and Bettie acknowledged bending the rules.

Bare Gulch [no date]
Monday Morning

Friend George,

For I am happy to be one of your friends. Yours of yesterday written on the bed came to hand last evening. I shall think of you often this summer keeping bachelor's hall, and sometime, when you get ready for me, I will come back to do your washing.

I am writing in the cart on my lap, for everything is packed but the stove. William has just returned from Searsville, the others are not ready: The consequence is, we shall not start until tomorrow…. please write so that I will get a letter when I get to Aurora, for we shall be sure to go there first.

Yours with respect,
Bettie G. Hughes

June 6th, 1862

Dear Friend Bettie,

I received your kind letter written in the *cart*… I didn't expect you would have time to write. I would like to hear how you are getting along and how you enjoy traveling. Does it make you seasick to ride in that old wagon? I think of you very often. I would like to happen along some night, just as you were all getting ready to camp for the night. I think it would be curious.

I expect when you write you will tell me all about it. I wish I had become acquainted with you before. I would have tried to make you stop to do my washing and not gone on that journey, but it was so short a time. I wanted to give you time to reflect, as well as myself. When I first saw you, I didn't take a fancy, but the more I have become acquainted, I like your appearance the more.

You may believe me; I am not writing this to flatter you. I write just what I mean. I am getting too old [28 years old] to be playing the fool, as most of young people will when they are younger than I am now and haven't seen so much of the world as I have. I know that they generally treat this subject too lightly. It is a serious one and should never be trifled with, as it generally causes a great deal of unhappiness between parties. I will leave this subject until I hear from you.

George.

George Washington Andrews, Crissie's father

[P.S.] I don't think George ever mistrusted that we sat up that night, nor [did] any of them.... I'm glad you didn't start until Tuesday, for it gave you time to get a good rest. I won't make you sit up all night again, but I didn't know when I should see you again, you were going so far.

Most respectfully
yours with true regard
from your friend,
Geo. W. Andrews

AURORA, 1862

New gold strikes were reported at Aurora in 1860. The Hughes family arrived in June of 1862, and one year later Aurora was a bustling town of 10,000 with 21 saloons, 20 stores, 12 hotels, 2 newspapers and 16 mills housing a total of 200 stamps that processed ore all day. Sam Clemens (not yet known as Mark Twain) tried his hand as a stamp mill laborer. Nevada and California squabbled over ownership of this remote boomtown named for the goddess of dawn. Lumber was scarce and many homes and businesses were constructed of brick and masonry.[1]

Aurora, [Nevada]
June 22nd 186[2]

Friend George,

We arrived in Aurora last Friday morning, tired and dirty, four weeks and five days on the road. People may say what they please about the novelty of traveling with an ox wagon. Some might like it but I don't. I can only think of it as a long, tedious journey. In the first place, our wagon was so large and long for the short turns on the mountain roads, everyone that met us would say, "Oh! You can't get down the mountain with that wagon," and it was all we could do. I held my breath sometimes, expecting to see everything go down the side of the mountain; and if it had, I think it would have been going yet, for it was down, down, as far as the eye could behold and a great *deal farther*.

You ask if it did not make me seasick. No, but it made me heartsick. You want to know how I like [it here], I presume. I have not seen much of the place yet, but I think if I was back there and knew as much as I do now, I would go out doing housework or *washing*—either—before I would come here, although they say it is a very good place for men to make money. We left Hunewill, Chat, and all the rest of them at Mond Springs, and they have not arrived yet.[2]

Bettie Hughes Andrews, Crissie's mother

George, I agree with you upon the subject of matrimony, for I don't believe in marrying in haste and repenting at leisure. I know that a great many think, if they are only married, that is the whole of life. They never seem to think of the long years of happiness or misery they must spend together until it comes, and then they blame each other for what they have to bear.

George, I know that you could never fancy me for my beauty, so that I have no fear of losing you when it fades. But if I have any good qualities that you can respect, I hope that I may always be deserving of that respect.

Bettie

In plainspoken, unromantic language, George and Bettie agreed to marry. The issues they discussed addressed some of the moral and social values of the 1860s West. How would they arrange their wedding, who would travel, and where would they meet? Should a man choose a woman based on beauty and social graces, or was her willingness to share hard work held in higher esteem? Labor by both husband and wife was required to make a living and raise a family in the West. Obviously, George valued a woman who was not afraid of the work ahead—hauling water, washing clothes by hand, preparing meals from scratch, building a home from the ground up, and raising children in an inhospitable environment. Restrictive social and religious rules of proper society were dropped of necessity.

Pescadero, [California]
July 1st, 1862

Friend Bettie,

I received your kind letter today... as I was going past the office, the clerk was standing in the door and said that there was a letter for me, and lo, it was from *(shall I say?) my* Bettie....

I'm both tired and sleepy—have been mowing hay all day, am hoeing and haying now. Have my potatoes nearly all hoed over. Getting along first rate. All I dislike is cooking. If I had someone to cook, I would be all right. I made some biscuits the other morning, the first I have made here. Threw in my soda and cream-a-tartar into a pan of flour with some milk. Got my hands all stuck over with dough, and the first thought? I was a mind to throw dough, pan, and all as far as I could throw it, but I took the second thought and rubbed my hands with flour and finished them, and they were quite good.

I was glad to hear that you arrived at the end of your journey so well as you did…. You said if I married you, it would not be for beauty. No, not at all the kind of beauty you mean. I don't think as many do [that] because a woman has a pretty face, that makes her a lady, by no means. I never intend to marry one for their beauty. I look more to the actions. If they act pretty, so pretty they are. A great many people would marry one with a pretty face, one that could sit in the parlor, play the piano, be a good singer—and be what some call a first-class lady. In my estimation they are not ladies that suit me. A woman that can cook a good meal of victuals, do up a shirt, and can take hold of anything that needs to be done without being afraid of soiling those pretty hands, can comfort the sick, and be kind to the poor, one that doesn't post themselves above common people—such people I like and ever respect.

…. If you think anything of me, speak the truth….

       Yours most affectionately &
       respectfully,
       Geo. W. Andrews

Pescadero, [California]
August 17th, 1862

Friend Bettie,

I received your letter mailed August 12th…. You said you wished you could coax me to come over there. But the way I'm situated at present, I cannot go very well. And besides, I think I can do as well here. From what I can learn, it is a more pleasant climate here and healthier, and I look at that a great deal in this world.

You said if you come this fall, you would have to come pretty soon on account of the winter…. You know that I want you to. I know that it belongs of me, and what belongs to true politeness, to go over there and get you, but do you wish me to do that? I know you are a noble traveler. You came to this country alone and performed a journey that a great many men are afraid to do. You can come just when it suits you. I shall leave it to you to say, and I will try to conform to your wishes.

I shall want to know when you are coming, that I may be prepared. I want to have you set the *happy* day and where you would like to get married. As I told you in my last, I think it just as well without a great ceremony…. Who would you like to be married by? Anyone will suit me except a *Catholic Priest*, and if you should want to select a priest, I should object. I know there is no danger of that. You are as much prejudiced as I am against *them*.

We can get the knot tied any place, almost. Shall leave it all to you, and it properly belongs to you…. Do you wish to go to keeping house as soon as you get married or how?

You asked me if I would always love you and stay at home with you evenings. I don't wish to marry unless I thought I could love you. And be assured, if I love my wife, I shall want to keep her company all that I can. I always thought it the place for a married man to be at home with his wife, when his business didn't call him elsewhere, for what is the use of being married unless they are at home?

The stage from Half Moon Bay comes in here now three times a week, so I can get mail oftener now.

       Yours truly,
       Geo. W. Andrews

Aurora, [Nevada]
August 24th, 1862

Dear George,

I received your kind letter of August 9th last Thursday... I think you are joking about the cooking; but if you like it, I am glad; for George, I have made up my mind to take you for better or worse, as poor as you say you are... and as for my coming here with the expectation of marrying a rich husband, if I started with any such expectations, really George, I was so seasick that I have forgotten it. I have always been poor, so it can be no great disappointment to remain so (although I do think it a big inconvenience) since it is nothing new, and if we have a good living and a home of our own and don't get very rich, I think we may still be happy and answer back, *I'll try*.

George, I think myself it is useless to spend all one has in getting married. I only wish to make a decent appearance. I shall get nothing much that is new, as I think my dresses are as good as I shall need to go into Pescadero society, and I presume we shall neither of us have any of our friends at our wedding. You did not say, but, of course, you will meet me in San Francisco.

Yours ever,
Bettie G.H.

P.S. George, please don't think that I am hurrying myself out [to] your hands, for I must write this plain if I come this fall, for I think it very doubtful if I am here long enough to receive an answer from this.

Aurora, [Nevada]
August 29th, 1862

Dear Friend George,

Your very kind letter of the 17th came to hand last night. George, you are very kind to offer to come over here after me, and I know that it would look better to other people. But it would cost a great deal for you to do so, and if you will think none the less of me, I am willing to meet you in San Francisco.... George, you may think it is not ladylike for me to offer to meet you, but I feel that what is your interest is mine now....

I am not particular in the choice of a clergyman. I think it best to go to keeping house as soon as we are married, and I think that will suit you, won't it? I cannot tell when I will leave here for certain, but if anything should happen that William should not come, I shall have to send my baggage on some other team and come myself in the stage.

George, please don't give me credit for so much amiability, for I am afraid that you will be disappointed, for I know that I have a great many faults.

Yours in Haste,
Bettie

Aurora, [Nevada]
September 10th, 186(2)

Dear George,

I have to tell you that my baggage left here for your side of the mountain this noon, and I am to follow in nine days. I think that I shall be in San Francisco Monday eve, September 22nd.

Oh! George I should feel bad enough if you should not meet me. But then you *will*, so I *will not* suppose such a thing.

If anything *should happen* that I should not get a letter from you or see you at the boat, I will take a carriage and go to the American Exchange.

I have ironed, packed my trunk, and finished my dress for the *occasion*. It is only a plain traveling dress. I will send you a little bit [swatch of dress material enclosed].

Yours as ever,
Bettie

EARLY MARRIED YEARS

George did receive Bettie's letter, and they were married September 24, 1862 in San Mateo, California, just south of San Francisco. Their first child—a son named Benjamin after George's father—was born nearly one year later, on August 16, 1863 at Woodside, California, which is located south and west of San Mateo.

The exact date of their move nearer to Nevada remains a mystery, but their trip would have taken them through Stockton and Calavares County on what is now Highway 4, through the Gold Rush country, then past Murphy's and Angel's Camp on the Big Trees Road.[2] Since George was an experienced lumber mill worker, perhaps he sought a mill job closer to the gold mining camps.

In the next letters, Bettie had set up housekeeping at Silver Mountain City, California, while George hauled lumber across Washoe Valley to the mines at Virginia City, Nevada.[3] George visited his family every few weeks, but did not return home to Bettie each night as he had once promised in his letters.

Twins, a daughter Laura and a son Byron (probably named for George's cousin) were born in October of 1864 when Benjamin was just a year old. Their love letters turned more toward daily accounts of their lives—George working long hours hauling lumber and supplies to earn the money his family needed, and Bettie working long hours to care for and feed three babies all under the age of two.

U.S. Census, 1860
Ragtown (later Reno) pop. 36 men, 2 women, 11 dwellings

Silver City, pop. 611 men, 25 women, 219 dwellings

Virginia City, pop. 2,198 men, 139 women, 808 dwellings

Washoe Valley (originally Wassau) pop. 200 men, 70 women, 60 dwellings

Washoe Valley deaths were as follows:
John Calvin, 29, typhoid fever, teamster
Senira Perkins, 16, typhoid fever
Louisa Perkins, 4, typhoid fever
Chester Barlow, 1, inflammation of bowels
Harriet Parks, 25, childbed
Thomas J. Owsley, 2, cholera infantum

Census & election of Districts of 1861
District No. 4, Silver City and vicinity. pop. 1,022

District No. 6, Virginia City and vicinity, pop. 3,284

District No. 7, Washoe, including the Washoe Valley and all the territory south of the divide between Washoe Valley and Steamboat Creek, pop. 1,005.

Source:

Thompson & West, *History of Nevada with Illustrations and Biographical Sketches of its Prominent Men & Pioneers*. Oakland, Cal.: Thompson & West, 1881.

HISTORY OF WASHOE COUNTY

Franktown, Wassau Valley, was founded on Feb. 22, 1857 as an agricultural area settled by a few Mormon farmers. The discovery of silver on Mount Davidson guaranteed a ready market for all the goods and services that residents of Washoe Valley could produce.

Gold Hill, Nevada. George earned a living by hauling lumber and supplies to Virginia City. His letters say that there are houses all the way from Gold Hill through Virginia City in 1865

"Thousands who came by this route passed through Washoe Valley, many of them stopping to avail themselves of the many peculiar advantages offered there by nature. Abounding in water, already well covered with farms and meadowlands, bordered on the west by mountains covered with a dense growth of pine and fir, the valley was ready for the hand of enterprise. The little town of Franktown, with its one sawmill, began to be of importance. The absence of both wood and water in the vicinity of the Comstock created great opportunities for a hauling business. Sawmills were built in the mountains, and the lumber and wood prepared there in great quantities was conveyed across the valley [to supply mines at Virginia City]. Produce of every kind from the farms, especially hay and barley, were also in great demand....

The population of this county began to increase.... Prospectors traversed it from one end to the other, and several mining districts were organized, and for a time held in great favor. The Argentine District in the mountains between the valley and Virginia City was organized in 1860, as was also the Galena District. The presence of water and fuel in such liberal quantities, led to the establishment of quartz mills.... The towns of Ophir, Washoe City and Galena all blazed up in 1861, and entered upon a career of prosperity that lasted several years. Ore was hauled across the barren mountains and the marshy ground at the head of Washoe Lake, and crushed at the several mills, and the teams returned with wood, lumber and produce, thus having a load both ways, and rendering the cost of getting the ore to the mill less than it would have been otherwise....

Washoe was one of the nine original counties into which the first Territorial Legislature divided the Territory of Nevada...

The seat of justice was located at Washoe City, the largest town at that time within its limits, at then less than a year of age.

The county offices were located and the first meetings of the Board were held in the Davis Building in Washoe City....

[and finally settled in] the Masons' brick building....

.... September 13, 1863, bids for building the jail were also advertised.... The buildings were completed and occupied before the end of the year.

The next half-dozen years saw great changes in Washoe County. In 1866, the wood and lumber business was of a most extensive character. Fifteen sawmills were constantly preparing lumber and mining timbers for the Comstock market, while hundreds of men were cutting cordwood for the use of the mills. These mills, most of them driven by steam-power, cut 1,300,000 feet of lumber per month, besides making thousands of feet of lath and shingles. This lumber was conveyed to Virginia and Gold Hill by the numerous freight wagons, which returned with loads of ore to be reduced in the quartz mills.... Washoe City, Ophir, Franktown and Galena were prosperous and busy.[4]

Among George and Bettie's daily details, their letters offer first-hand impressions of the communities born to feed the Comstock's hungry appetite for wood and supplies. They wrote about the price of flour and cloth, the dates and infrequency of shipments of supplies, the fashions and fun at social gatherings, and the work—always the work. Through it all, their optimism and obvious love for each other seemed strong enough to conquer any hardships.

Virginia City, Sunday night

Dear Bettie,

Here I am. Arrived in town with my load of poles all the way from Washoe City. I told you in my last I was hauling here. Well, it's about 9 o'clock now. I've eaten my supper and fed my cattle the second time. Am ready to go to bed, but I thought I would just say a word to my Bettie. I would like to have you here, but no use talking of impossibilities. I hope we will sleep under the same roof ere long. I have made up my mind where to build, if I can get the chance, and probably will commence it by the last of this week.

I priced some flour tonight. Was 7 dollars per hundred. I think I will get some. Syrup 7½ cents per gallon. Brown sugar 18 cents per box....

Well, my load of poles comes to $60 clean cash. Pretty good. It was a pretty hard drive, but I feel as if I was obliged to make some good licks now to get even. Teaming is going to be good here pretty soon. I think they have struck it in the Gould & Curry, richer than ever, 450 feet deeper than they have ever been before. So is the report. If true, business will

Benjamin Howard Andrews, Crissie's brother

be better than ever.

I want you here. Perhaps I may be at home by week from Saturday, but don't know certain, which will be two weeks. I hope you won't faint if I should take you by surprise, for I can't tell what time I may start. But if I should I fail to come in two weeks, now don't pine all away.

        Good night, kiss the
        babies,
        George

Washoe City, Nevada
June 12th, 1865

Dear Bettie,

I suppose you will be looking anxiously for a line from me, as you are all alone with the little ones. I have nothing particular to write. I sent you a line as I went through Genoa to tell you about the corn meal. I suppose you got it. I went through Carson City, stopped there, got dinner. Couldn't get any job there. It is quite a little town, though dull. Went through Empire, which is a one-horse town. Nothing going on there.

We got into Dayton about 9 o'clock that eve; we looked around there until about 9 the next day but struck nothing. Quite a number of quartz mills, which support the place. We started for Gold Hill, which is about six or eight miles. Passed through Silver City, which lays in the same canyon. The place appears just like a factory town at home [New Hampshire] composed of quartz mills and boarding houses and little houses for one family to live in. One would say that Gold Hill and Silver City were all one—for four miles the gulch is lined with mills and houses. There were about half of them running.

Times were dull. When you get to the top of the hill, you can see Virginia [City, early letters refer to Virginia City as simply Virginia], or you might say you had arrived there, for these three places are all connected by buildings. We had found nothing yet, so we proceeded to this place. Got here about dark Thursday eve. Friday went to the sawmills. Could get one job this week. Saturday worked for a man hauling wood. Yesterday went to look at a wood-hauling job. If I had my team here, I could get three or four jobs, but teamsters complain of low prices. If I had them here, I could make a living. This is the best place I have struck yet. There are over a hundred teams coming in and passing to Virginia City and Gold Hill daily. I shall come up and get my team as soon as I can, or get a part of it. Can use two or three yoke here and make $8 or $10. Dan sold his mare and colt to the Indians. Is spreeing it a little.

I'm stopping with a real old Irish gentleman bachelor. I got some meat at the butcher and cooked it—and bread at the bakery—so I have no one to dictate or to be dictated.... I believe this is a good place for teaming, and I think you would like it. There are three quartz mills in this place. I must close, the stage goes out at 8 o'clock. If you write, direct [letters] to this place: Washoe City, Nevada. I'm well. Hope you are the same. Keep in good spirits; we can make a living here. A kiss to you and the babies. I think of you all often.

        Yours with affection,
        George

I send you a [news]paper.

Silver Mountain [City, California]
June [1865]

Dear Father,
 Now Mother is going to write you a good long letter all about Sonny [nickname for Benjamin] and the little twins. It seems a long time since you left us, and yet the days seem short. I am so busy feeding and taking care of my babies and wondering what Father is doing now.
 Oh, by the way, R... just brought me in a sample of his cooking, a saucer of brains. (You say a splendid dish.) I waited till he had gone out. I was afraid I couldn't eat it, but Ben and I ate it all up, and Ben wanted more.
 The little scamp crawled under the house to where I had a hen's nest and broke all the eggs. He whistles round and tries to put on Father's boots. Says, "Where'd Garge go?" Laura is playing with her toes. I asked what Mammy should tell Father. She says, "hug." Byron is asleep. I have got my washing and ironing done for this week.
 Now George, I have told you everything except to say I love you and wish I was down there with you, then I'd give you good substantial proof, wouldn't I? Now write often. Laura and Mother send a kiss. She is laughing and talking away, but Mother doesn't understand a word she says.
        From your own true & faithful,
        Bettie
This is the last envelope the house affords.

Washoe City, [Nevada]
June 1865

Dear Bettie & little ones,
 I received yours Saturday. You say you felt lonesome. It is no more so with you than it is with me....
 I commenced boarding at the hotel, pay eight dollars per week. I must have a square meal when I work here, but [they] don't pay very big—about the same as the Redwoods.... I hear of jobs every day. I think as soon as I can, I will come up and get the rest of my team, and we will move down here. There are places near town that I could put a cabin on. There are not many very good buildings here and rent is high, $10 to $20 per month.

Wells Fargo receipt

I can get lumber for $15 per m. [a meter, or 39.37 inches] so it won't cost much to build a cabin. I would like a place near the lake [Washoe Lake], and then we can raise a garden. There is plenty of ground that is good, all common, if I can get it; and it could be irrigated from the lake very easy by having a windmill. There is a breeze here most every day that would drive it.

Do you have grub enough? You must be pretty short. Tell me in season. I will send you some money as soon as I can, but you must tell me. I think of you and the little ones often and feel most ashamed that I'm in this fix, but we will keep good courage. I think we may conquer sometime. Oh, if you were here to give me a sample of your love now. Good night. I will go and get my supper now—can get meals from 5 a.m. till 10 p.m.

Yours thoughtfully
and faithfully,
G. W. Andrews

Washoe City, [Nevada]
July 1st, 1865

Dear Bettie,

I just received a letter from you. It came rather unexpected. I was right glad to get it, and I hasten now with pleasure to write you a line, as I know you are watching with anxiety each mail.... I'm writing this at the P.O. They keep this paper for people, gratis, so I improve the opportunity. I was glad to hear you were so well, and the little ones.

I would like to have you keep a diary of your life. I think no doubt it would sell well. It is about as warm here as it is over at Woodside... and as dusty. I turned my cattle in a pasture tonight, have to pay 25 cents per head, but if I keep on teaming, I must keep my cattle in good order.

I wish I had some money to send you now, but if you feel in need of any thing, tell me—don't go needy more than possible.... don't think hard if I don't write so often. I love you the same as if I wrote every mail.

Kiss the little ones for me.
From George

Silver Mountain, [California]
July 2nd, 1865

Dear Father,

I haven't much news to write, only to say we are pretty

well, all but Laura. She isn't very smart—cutting her teeth, I guess. Old fatty [Bettie's nickname for Byron] is all right, and Bennie hasn't forgot to say George yet, nor has Mammy forgot to think of him.

Well, Father, Byron is grunting. I have some gruel to make.... I hope it will be so you can send me some money.... Five dollars will be enough. If I take that up at Powers, I shall have to have some to pay the milkman. I haven't quite a half sack of flour, little more than enough to last me this week. I put some pockets in Old Longs pants, and he gave me some carrots and parsnips. They are too old to be very good—some like him. Byron positively declares he won't stand it any longer

Monday
Dear George,

I will finish your letter now. It is raining, so I didn't wash.

Bennie gave me a kiss. I'll send it to you with one of my own and one for the babies. George, don't build a house where it will be out of the way for you, for perhaps we won't live there a great while. Anyway, make a room the size of that room of R's with a chamber and woodshed. No need of a partition. I'll use that same curtain. It's cheaper than anything else. One fire will warm bedroom and kitchen, save lumber and paper; use chamber and shed for storeroom. The paper you sent me, I sent home to B. Andrews. My little Bennie has gone to sleep on his pillow in front of the stove. Write to us on Sundays and think of us every day.

      God bless you my darling,
      From Bettie Andrews

Washoe City, [Nevada]
July 6, 1865

Dear Bettie & little ones,

I have just received a letter from you, and one from Hat [Harriet] enclosed in it. I was glad to hear from you and them, too. Then William is going to ranching, if he finds one. I'm glad to hear that he has done so well.... Hat spoke that it would be pleasant to live near, that we might see one another once in a while. It would be pleasant. Nothing would suite me better than to live among my friends, but while I'm so poor, I don't want to see anyone, or at least I feel so. I shall get some money Saturday and will send it by Wells Fargo & Co.'s express. I will put it in Sunday morning, so you will get it Monday, I think, or Wednesday certain. I will send to Mrs. Geo. W. Andrews, $20 or $25. If you should want any before you get mine, perhaps Old Long may let you have a little for a day or two. I would like to be there when William comes.

      Good night
      G.W.A.

Mill at Virginia City, Nevada

Washoe City, [Nevada]
July 7th, 1865

Dear Bettie,

I received a letter from you and one enclosed in it from Hat and also a story.... You sent the story thinking our love had demised some? I can say mine has not, but I've so much to do to gain a living, I'm obliged to pay my attention to that more. I have no doubt, if we had a fine house, horses, carriage, and plenty of means, we would be as happy as the doctor in that story. But how can I do so much, when I have to put in every moment I have to get a living?

.... I know we have some times that are not quite so pleasant, but we may see a good time, if our luck should turn. It is impossible for me to live truly happy so long as I am d---d poor. The main thing is to study to please, trying to conform to each other's wishes as much as possible; and if we try, perhaps we can be like the doctor's folks.

Today is Sunday. I thought I would let my team rest today, and myself too, but I've been busy most of the time. I salted my cattle this forenoon, and this afternoon I've done my washing. I haven't washed any before today. I had quite a string of wash. I wished Bettie was here then, though perhaps I had as much time as she; and besides, I went into the lake and had a good swim myself, which one needs after being in the dust a whole week through.

We had a nice rain the 3rd. I had just gone up in the mountain after my load... and also worked on the 4th. There was not much going on here. They had an oration (some say it was good) and some fireworks (some say they were good), but it would delight me just as much to watch sparks coming from a stovepipe in a dark night. They had quite a large ball, a splendid ball, and seven- or ten-set dance at once. I didn't go, but it is on the ground, so one can look in as they pass by. The ladies were tolerably well dressed... mostly in summer clothing, while the gents dressed about the same as in California. You shouldn't have been mortified when cousin caught you hoopless, for I think that some didn't have on hardly any hoops, if any. They were, or appeared to be, mostly modest ladies, so I didn't seek for inspection. I saw them dance two cotillion... one fancy dance, and then I went to bed. They don't dance here much different than in California. They are to have a circus next Thursday.

I sent you twenty-five dollars by Wells Fargo & Co. Express.... I paid the charges on it, so all you have to do is to ask for it. I could have sent you a smaller sum when I wrote you last but knew you needed more.

I guess I will close, for I have to grease my wagon, ready for an early start in the morning.... A kiss to you and the babies all round, and I will close.

Yours as ever with true
love and affection,
Geo. W. Andrews

Silver Mountain [City, California]
July 6, 1865

Dear Father,

I received a letter from your home Monday and am going to send it with this. I took the liberty to read it.... I feel well paid for letting your mother know where you were and that you're *alive and well, I hope.*

Geo, I have got to have a bedstead, so Old Long said he'd borrow me one. (Old Long is my right-hand mower now.) I would sleep on the floor, but I'd get the bedclothes so dirty. Bennie would be on it all the time and dirty the blankets so.

I had some fish for my supper. Ralf got some and brought them, (gave me half of three) for me to fry. Had no lard or meal.

It's 11 o'clock, and I've the babies to feed. I wish I could go to bed to you instead of sitting up writing to you. We're all well. Bennie is full of mischief. The little ones are clever, fat, and sweet. I am tired and sleepy.

George, I'm glad to hear you speak so cheerful, for I think you feel it, and glad you can have a square meal. I'll finish now for tonight. Will perhaps write some more tomorrow. Good night.

Friday.

I received the Almanac and envelopes. I'm much obliged, but I had bought some of my own. Oh! George, I never saw anything so rich as THL [mine]. The old woman brought in a piece. You can see the native silver all through its cavities in the quartz (it looks like fruit on the windows) all filled with it, and they say it's plenty. It looks pretty.

Now to my own business. Powers asks $5 a sack for flour. The rest are selling for $4 and $4.50 (all I've heard of). I hope you can send me some money. I'll let the milkman take that. I've had nine gallons of milk; it runs up pretty fast...

From your true and loving wife,
Bettie Andrews

P.S. Bennie is saying George

Silver Mountain [City, California]
July 15th, 1865

Dear Father,

I went up to Mrs. Thompson's yesterday to get a pattern for Bennie, a dress. She keeps the Emporium of fashions in this town. She's just made herself and Mrs. Adams some bonnets. They think they're beautiful.... but look as if somebody made them themselves.

The little creek has given out. I have to go to the big one now. I've got one tub of water towards doing my washing. Aren't I pretty smart? And I've a pretty little bouquet of wild roses and grass that I picked myself over at the creek.

I thought I never would get ready (Sunday 4 o'clock) to say a word to you today. Something kept me busy since six this morning, but I've got my wash water—I brought some this morning and gave a Piute a biscuit to bring the rest. Wasn't I in luck? We had quite a rain yesterday, or several showers, and it's storming all day today on the summit. It has come as far down as that green patch—you know where we went to ride—but not quite here.

.... You had better bring your blankets when you come after us. I expect it will be better for us to sleep in the wagon. The babies and Ben will want to go to bed before you're ready to stop at night, and it would be such a job to get them all out so early in the morning; so if they are already there, we'll have nothing to do but hitch up and start. You said you didn't know when you'd come. If your time comes any where near mine, I should like for you to come then, or I'll have to make you wait.

I put the little twins in wash dresses today. Laura is as full of tickle as she used to be since she's got two teeth. She likes to hear them on the cup when she's drinking. Ben has kissed this sheet all over to send to Geo. He found your mittens this morning in that box and came out with them on his hands saying, "Here's George." He hadn't forgot. Old fatty Byron remains the same, fat and clever. If you were here, I'd give you something better than a kiss good night.

From you ever true and faithful,
Bettie

Washoe City, [Nevada]
Sunday, July 16th, 1865

Dear Bettie,

I have been one trip to Virginia City since I wrote. I'm hauling some poles to the Ophir mine and will go two or three trips more. My team travels like horses. I beat one mule team in. I started from here, intending to stop at the Summit house about 4½ miles from Virginia City; but on getting there so early at 3 p.m., I thought I would go in town, and it was cloudy and looked as if it would rain, and it did rain the other side of the Carson. My load would have hauled heavy had it rained, so I made my little steers trot. Got in Virginia City about 7 p.m. Got stuck pretty near the mine: was directed wrong. It is bad hillsome streets, so after some cursing and swearing—you can imagine how I appeared, but I was a stranger to them and I didn't care. But the people there were very kind to me when they saw me in trouble. Several offered to assist me... one woman among the rest. She blocked the wheel for me when she saw my cattle couldn't hold it.... I told her I guessed she'd been a bull driver before. She laughed and said no, but her husband was, so she knew something about teaming. So I stopped in Virginia City that night and fed my cattle.

I have a better job than hauling wood. My freight came to $39. It took me two (or three?) days to make the trip. I have a load... which will amount to $68, and better than all, my money is counted out to me when I take my load off. I feel better when I'm making something. I mean to clear a $100 this week, if I can. If you were here to cook my grub, I could do it. It would be so pleasant. I must tell you there is no place like home. I'm a great deal happier when I'm with you, notwithstanding our little broils we have once in awhile, just for a change. All just for fun. We'll laugh and say so, won't we? Don't get impatient. I'm as anxious to have you here as you are to come.

I thought I would write home [to his parents] today, but haven't time. I must write to those whom I love and are dear to me first. I was glad you put in a word [to my parents] in that [news]paper. I love you for it. I think of my people at home [in New Hampshire] a great deal, but say little. I think of them many times and wish that we might go and see them and for them to return the visit. It would be so pleasant to give them a concert of our house organs. I think we could teach Mary sheet music, although she plays in the schoolroom. I would be happy to have you write to them....

Flour is $4.25 per sack in Virginia City. I went through part of one of the principle streets after I got my supper, and I was astonished at what stores they had. Dry good's, I should think, would be as cheap as in San Francisco, nearly. The stores appear as rich as in S.F.

Don't forget to kiss the babies for me.

Yours in truth from your,
George

Silver Mountain City, California
July 20th, [1865 probably]

Dear Father,

George, it gives me pleasure to have you say there's no place like home, so I think—it's my world. If that wasn't a pleasant place, I should have no pleasure anywhere. I don't care for parties and balls and what they call society. When we get able, I'd like a few friends, but we'll talk of that some other time. I'll not go hungry, be sure of that.

George, you'll come, and that's more to me than if everyone else came [to visit on their way to California from Aurora.] Sister Syrene is married out South, you will see by Sister Jane's letter. This teacher here used to know Syrene. He taught school in Bath, [Maine]. He became acquainted with her at the Teachers' Institute. Rachel has gone up river to keep school. That's our-half sister you know: I have another younger than Esther.

I kiss the babies every time I take them up for you, and you'll find aplenty sent back, if you look sharp. George, guess I must be writing too often. My stamps are nearly gone....

Yours as ever from,
Bettie & the Babies,

with love to Father

Silver Mountain City, California
July 23, 1865

Dear George,

… It seems we never had so many letters. This one from your sister [Martha] (received Friday after I'd mailed your last), I think, contains most excellent news. It seems that she, too, has found a husband. She has experienced religion since we heard from her before. She seems very happy in her new-found treasures. If she is so rich now, what will she think when she gets a pair of twins? Father, she hasn't but just begun to get rich.

I must go hunt up Ben. He picks all the mullen around for bouquets. He's come with the water dipper full of chips. He is getting so he can talk quite plain. I think Byron will split his lungs if I don't take him up.... I must begin to hurry up, or I won't have the babies ready when you come. I hope it'll be soon.

Your own dear,
Bettie

Washoe City
July 28th, 1865
Dear Bettie,

I'm hauling poles for the mines; get $1.50 apiece. Have hauled sixty-six, and two loads, and Sunday I will have forty more in, [that] will make 106, [and] will be $139. I told you I meant to clear $100 this week. I can get jobs every day.

You are anxious to know when I'm coming. I can't tell you in this letter, but hope I will before long. I want money to get grub and to build my cabin and to get you down here. … A great many people are about discouraged about Virginia [City].... A great many are leaving and will go as soon as they can.

I'm told everything is pretty cheap there. Flour is $7.50 per hundred, $3.75 per sack; sugar, 5 lbs. per $1.00; calicoes, two and three bits per yard; flannel, five bits to seven; potatoes, 10 cents per lb. retail, new ones. I priced some things when I was there. I had a little time evenings. Can get furniture as cheap as in San Francisco now on account of dull times, but one would think times were pretty good to go through town.

You said you had to pack your water from the big creek—it's too bad. I wish you were here, then I'd do it and the rest of the little chores, you know. But it will do you good to go out, not stay in the house all the time. The time you said it rained, I don't suppose you thought I was getting a good ducking. Everyone appeared in the road to welcome it; notwithstanding they were getting a good soaking.

I think of you when I look at Silver Peak lying just above you within 2½ or 3 miles of you. I can see it plain as I pass over the summit to Virginia [City]. It would be so nice to have a drink of good cool water and to be with

Bettie. She would make me eggnog when it was so hot, and give me good victuals and everything that's good. I carry lunch with me on the road. They charge 75 cents a meal. I get my dinner put up here, which lasts me to Virginia [City]. I got a can of peach jam and a loaf of bread, which last me back again, and I can eat when I get hungry. Well, Bettie, it is getting dark now, and I will say good night.

                                     Love the little ones for me,
                                     From your Husband
                                     George

Washoe City
July 30th, 1865

Dear Bettie,

I priced some calicos in Virginia [City] the last time I was there. They were 3 bits per yard—French goods, they called them. They didn't look so good a quality as the last dress I got you, but in the night I couldn't tell. I don't think I can be at home next Saturday. It is Sunday today, but the last of the next week I think I'll be poking along. I've lost some flesh, but I feel first rate. A good many are complaining about being sick—drink too much water I guess. I carry my keg and fill it in the mountains and get splendid water. I must close. Remember me to the babies.

                                     From Geo. W

Washoe City, [Nevada]
Aug 6th, 1865

Dear ones at home,

Or I'll address you *"Mother"* as you do me Father. I don't think you have ever been called by that name before. How does it seem? Well, we've got to stand it now: it is so. We are parents now, and by the laws of nature, we cannot get away from it…. When I told you the time before the last that I would start the first, but I struck a paying job, so I stopped a little longer. I will be at home a week from today, or Monday the 13th I think now. I want to bring my lumber for the house tomorrow, and the carpenter will go at work on it. He has been changing works with another carpenter, and the two will go at work on it.

I just got home from a trip to Virginia [City] last night. I bought my windows there, four for $11. The doors, the carpenter is to make, and build the house for $35.00. I get my lumber at the mill for $15. I bought bbl. [a barrel of] flour, $14; sugar, lard, corn meal and rye; box of soda and some other trinkets.

Yes, if you want that sewing machine, get it. You need something of that kind, and it will do till we are able to get a better one or till Laura wants one. If she's smart, she will want one in a year or two. Is it in running order? They cost $25 when I was at Searsville.

I didn't feel very well going to Virginia [City], had some diarrhea. Am better now, and I will go up to the mill and stay tonight. It costs $1.30 per night to keep my cattle in pasture, no feed outside.

Tell Mr. Neeley that carpenters are in good demand at Virginia [City] now, wages $3.00 per day. Carpenters tell me so. Men are scarce here just now, as the farmers are haying. Crew had to shut down his mill at Empire. The men struck for $4 per day. Times are going to be good here this fall, everyone says. I hauled a load to the Gould & Curry mine. The freight came to $53.

If you were here just now, you might have a laugh. A lot of the boys in town, six or seven, are out sailing on the lake and have capsized the sailboat, and they are all in the water up to their armpits trying to upright their boat again.

Remember the babies for me,

      From your
      Geo.

George did move Bettie and the children from Silver Mountain City to Washoe Valley, soon after that last letter.

Then tragedy struck. The twins, Laura and Byron, died sometime around the time of the move to Washoe Valley. Did the babies die of illness, either from contaminated water at Silver Mountain City or some contagious disease such as cholera or typhoid? In an earlier letter, George reported being sick with diarrhea, and he mentioned that others in Washoe Valley and Virginia City were sick from the drinking water. Perhaps they died from an accident during the move to Washoe City. No one will ever know, because the twins were never again mentioned by name in any of the letters. Crissie told me they are buried in the Washoe Valley cemetery, but none of us remembers exactly where the tiny graves are located.

Only parents who have experienced the death of a child can possibly understand the heartache that came into George and Bettie's marriage. The few letters written between them after August 1865 seem to be written by two people who were very different from the young lovers in the earlier letters. George and Bettie carried on after that tragic loss, but the heaviness that was in their hearts seeped into their correspondence and eventually into their relationship. In taking their children, the West handed the couple a pain that not even their love for each other could cure.

Washoe City
September 9, 1870

Well my dear,

I have been waiting all week expecting you to write that you had struck a big thing, but I knew all the time it wasn't there. That place is over done and unless you *have a dead sure thing*, I shall not *Move* this fall, for I know that we shall be moving away from home. George, I can't make up my mind. When I think of it I feel as if I were going to a funeral. George, you are just as likely to get a job here as there after the mill starts, but you won't see it…. I know the fall is no time to move and build when money is so scarce… I don't think teaming is going to pay this winter anywhere… now don't be cross, for I think before next spring you will be glad if we don't change. I wish you could be home. It is lonesome here.

George, I have given up getting rich…. Well, I know you will be tired of this…. I had a letter from Sister Rachel this morning, I will enclose with mine… I will do what I can for her to get the school.

Good night. Tell me if this is a pleasant letter. Crissie says she sleeps in Pappy's chaise.

Bettie Andrews

Reno
Sunday, October 18, 1874

Dear Bettie,

I came to Reno today. I did not go up in the mountains this week…. I saw Mr. [Orvis] Ring, the county superintendent. He said they had a teacher at Franktown engagedf or a year. The teacher at Washoe, they had hired for three months only. Didn't know as they wanted school in winter, he said. Didn't know when there would be a vacancy. When there was, he would give her [Bettie's sister Rachel] a show, if she were here. I suppose Martha is gone by this time. I will be home next Sunday.

Love to you all – in
haste from,
George

CHAPTER THREE
Crissie's Aunts and Uncles

THE HUGHES FAMILY

BETTIE HUGHES was one of eight children, and she maintained contact through letters with most of her brothers and sisters throughout her life. I traced the Hughes family back to the Kennebec River area of Maine. They apparently lived at Madison in Kennebec County and Skowhegan in nearby Somerset County, Maine.[1] Kennebec was settled in 1799 according to the Kennebec Historical Society, and in 1800 had a population of 1,216. By the time the Hughes siblings headed west in the 1850's the population was 7,609. The Hughes family tree has been drawn based on information taken from their letters. Bettie's parents were John and Syrena Hughes. Records show that John Hughes was in the Kennebec County jail in October 1837 for "debt." Bettie would have been about 3 years old at the time. John and Syrena both died at relatively young ages. Syrena died at age 41. John remarried, but about six years later he drowned at age 47 in 1847.[i2]

Bettie was born in 1834 at Skowhegan and raised at Madison. John's first family had four girls and two boys – William, Bettie, John, Jane (Mary Jane, known to me as Aunt Jane Powell), Stella (always called Hannah) and Syrene. After Syrena's death, John remarried and his second wife was Rhoda Briggs. At least two more girls were born to this marriage, Esther and Rachel.[3]

The earliest letters from the Hughes family date back to August 4, 1855 and were addressed simply to "Sister" from John C. Hughes.[4] At that time, the siblings were evidently scattered by the family's poverty. The sisters lived with other families and worked for room and board, while brother John worked to set up his own business. Their greatest hope was that brother William in California would strike it rich and return to help them.

Boston
April 10th, 1856

Dear Sister,
    I have been trying for a long time to get time to write to you... in your last letter you were rather low-spirited, and I don't know as I can blame

William Hughes, Bettie's brother and Crissie's uncle

Harriet Hughes, William's wife and Crissie's aunt. Crissie's middle name is Harriet, named for this aunt

you for it, but you must keep up good spirits for one year longer, if you can, and then William will be home, and we will try and do something so that you and Jane won't have to work so hard, for I am in hopes that we can go into some kind of business for ourselves.

I had a letter from William the last mail, but no.... I don't know as I am sorry that he has concluded to stay another year, for he can do better there than he can here, and every thing is so high here now....

From your brother
John C. Hughes

[letterhead says "Fillmore is the man"]

Boston
October 13th, 1856

Dear Sister,

You must excuse me for not writing to you before, but I have had so much to do.... I have to work Sundays and all. My health is very good now.... I have got almost over my lameness... I should like to come up there and see you and Jane, but I can't till next summer anyway...

P.S. Sister, I was just going down to the post office with this, when who should walk in but brother William, right from California, and perhaps I wasn't glad to see him, and then again perhaps I was. He looks just as he did when he went away. He hasn't changed one mite. Yes, he has got home and has got married before he left there.... I did not see his wife, but he said that she is mighty handsome and rich too....

J.C. Hughes

According to family folklore, sisters Bettie and Syrene were the next Hughes to head west. However, Syrene met and married a colorful man from Alabama—a Confederate soldier named "Pick" Clark, who had lost a leg in the Civil War. Syrene remained in Alabama for the rest of her life, and Bettie continued to San Francisco to be with her brother, William Hughes. She traveled the rest of the journey alone.

Eventually, two younger sisters also went west. Hannah married Moses Hearne; they had a son, and she was a well-known nurse at Bodie, California. Napoleon Bonaparte Hunewill did strike it rich and returned to Maine to marry Esther Ann Hughes. The couple traveled west together, spent some time with William and his wife Harriet, traveled with them to Aurora, and then settled a ranch at Bridgeport, California, that is still operated by descendants of the Hunewill family. Today it is the Hunewill Guest Ranch, a popular summer vacation spot. One of the youngest sisters, Rachel, followed later and taught school at Aurora and possibly at Washoe City.

Napoleon Bonaparte Honeywell, one of five brothers who settled near Kennebec River, Maine, sailed via Cape Horn for California in 1852 and mined around Marysville, Grass Valley, Nevada City, Placerville, and Downieville along the Yuba River. Napoleon made his fortune by 1859 and returned to Maine to marry Esther Anne Hughes, sister of Bettie Hughes.

Esther's brother Will and his wife Harriet went to California with them, this time crossing the Isthmus... "the women rode mules or donkeys, while the men walked."

In California, William and Napoleon purchased a sawmill at Woodside, south of San Francisco. Esther's son Frank Eugene Hunewill was born there. In the spring of 1861 [or 1862, discrepancy in dates], floods demolished the mill. The Civil War was starting back east and there were new mining camps in Nevada. William, Napoleon, and their families went to Aurora in two wagons with yoked oxen – over the Sierra, ascending through Placerville, past Lake Tahoe, down Kingsbury Grade to Carson Valley, past Mormon Station (Genoa). The men visited Virginia City, but continued across the Carson River at Cradelbaugh's Bridge, through present-day Minden and Gardnerville to Aurora in Esmeralda Gulch.

Aurora needed lumber, so Napoleon followed the Walker River and homesteaded the Hunewill Ranch on Robinson and Buckeye Creeks. There he built the Eagle Creek Mill in 1862. He helped settle Bridgeport, county seat of Mono County in 1864. Esther and Napoleon built a big ranch house and brought furniture in from San Francisco. Their son Frank married Alice Hyde, and they lived with Napoleon and Esther and were parents of Lucile, Camille (Millie), and Stanley.

During the Great Depression in the 1930s, the Circle H was turned into a guest ranch.

Hamblet, Millie Hunewill. *The Saga of the Circle H, 1861 - 1961.*

LETTERS FROM AURORA

William's wife, Harriet, wrote long, newsy letters to Bettie and George from Aurora, the mining camp near the California-Nevada border that flourished for a few short years in the early 1860s. Harriet described in wonderful detail the economy, weather, social events, and activities of some of the town's colorful citizens. Perhaps, Harriet fit right into the mining camp, because Jane said in one of her letters that "Harriet has made such a good resolution and hope she will stick to it, for there is no good that comes of card playing...." I loved Aunt Harriet's gossipy Aurora letters.

January 1, 1863

I wish you a happy New Year. I have got something pretty good to tell you. Mrs. Hanson and Mr. Crocker have had a falling out. Mrs. Codington and myself went in there. Mrs. H. threw a chair at him and then took the broom to him. I thought it was time for me to leave, but Mrs. C. stopped to see it out.

Mrs. Hanson came up and told the story after they left. She says Crocker has been making love to her all summer. I think she would not have told of it, if we had not happened in there as we did, unfortunately for her. By the way,

Uncle William's house in Aurora, 1920

Hanson was out to the Meadows. (He is a very fine man indeed, just as fine a man as this world affords.)

The military had a ball here the fourth of last month. There were about 100 gents and fifty ladies. We went and had a nice time. The firemen had one on Christmas Eve.... The riflemen have built a large hall about half way up the hill on the road to the graveyard.

I must tell you, we had the old Shang Hi rooster for Christmas dinner. Esther and Hunewill, Kidd and Noris, Peter Gambril and Forrest were here to dinner, and we had a good time, generally.

Napoleon Bonaparte Hunewill

Esther Hughes Hunewill, Bettie's sister and Crissie's aunt

Esther Hughes Hunewill, 1888

The Hunewill Ranch at Bridgeport, California

By the way, Noris is out of the Wide West [name of a mining claim]. Speaking of the Wide West puts me in mind of the Waterman Ledge. The men have had some work done on it. William says tell you your assessments do not amount to over one $100.... I think it is not much account, but we can't tell yet.

Mrs. Codington and myself received those patterns you sent. By the way, I sent you a letter we received from Jane, and I hope you have answered it, for we have not….. Write as soon as convenient…. I made Mrs. Codington a black silk and Mrs. Moulton one for the ball. Our love to all, George and yourself in particular…. one more thing I have to say—if you need that buff dress, don't be bashful, but say so and you shall have it. I shall have a good chance to send it in the spring with William.

Harriet

[Undated, possibly autumn 1863]
Well Bett,

In the first place, I must tell you we are all well…. Hunewill folks are well. They have gotten into their house about two weeks ago, but it is not half done yet. Esther and Frank [Bettie's sister Esther and her son Frank] were here last Thursday visiting. We have our house all fixed up. It is partitioned off, and I have two windows in front and the comfort down, and it is so warm that I am obliged to open the door when I have a fire.

I would feel first rate if William was at home, but he is teaming to the Meadows, and the Indians have become very troublesome. They stopped Cale and made him deliver up his blanket and grub and money… then said they would kill him, snapped their gun, but it did not go off. He then ran and they left him. He went back and got his team. I think he was some scared. They robbed three others the same day in that place. It was two miles from White's ranch. The teamsters go well armed now, but I can't help being worried all the time William is gone. He has sold his team and is driving it by the month, and if he drives next summer, he will go over to the woods in the spring and get him up another.

The Sacks family have gone to Oakland to live, and Flora is stopping here. She conducts herself as well as any lady in town. She is stopping with Mrs. Codington now. She went to church today with her for the first time since you left. She told me she had applied for a divorce, and she was going to marry Harry Newton in the spring. Mark Gage is here now, but he is going to Carson to stop this winter. Codington has gone to San Francisco. He went the next week after you did and has not returned yet. They have rented a little brick house for this winter just below here.

There have been many buildings put up on this hill since you left. Moulton's folks have moved in to this little cabin next to us. They are going to build just across the street from there. I think Mr. Hanson has not got the money yet, for Mrs. Hanson is in a bad way. She thinks they can't get in their winter's provision, and I think going over the mountain is played out. I think I shall not be alone this winter, for I do not know any one who is going to leave, and there were a great many families that came in this fall.

By the way, I must tell you—Tarp of San Mateo came over about three weeks ago, and for about two weeks he was drunk. William took him out to the Meadows to get him sobered off, and while he was gone, his wife came over. Frank Nielson is here. He came last week. He said he saw George Fillbrick in Carson. He says he is making money very fast and is going to Searsville to pay all he owes there. Perhaps that will be interesting to George Andrews, for I believe he owes him some.

You said you would like me to have some of your nice tomatoes and potatoes. The tomatoes I should like very much. We have plenty potatoes. They are only seven cents per pound.

I am glad you enjoy yourself so well and have such a nice husband. I would like to have you both come over here, but I should much rather go over there. Give our love to all, Chandilers' folks in particular.

Goodbye for the present.
Harriet

Tell George the agreement about that buff dress was for him. So write to me if you need it, and I shall barter an extra express to take it there directly.

Crissie and Millie Hunewill with donkey at Wellington. Millie wrote the book about the Hunewill Ranch at Bridgeport

Aurora
December 28, 1863

Well Bett,

I suppose by this time you would like to hear from Aurora and hear if we are all frozen in here; but I can tell you, we have had some very fine weather so far—a little snow, but none to stay on the ground any length of time. We are all well, and I feel better contented than I did in the summer. It has been very sickly here this fall and several deaths. Mrs. Price died about six weeks ago and left four little children—the youngest, one week old. Mrs. Rogers has it now. (She says tell Mrs. Bettie she wishes her much joy with her little boy, and tell her she has a daughter.)

By the way, I had almost forgotten to tell you, I have one of them myself—a little girl two and a half years old. Mrs. Hanson has the other girl, older. I tell you Betty, I always was down on young ones but.... not...now. The Father thinks he will take them to the states in the spring.

And now for the news. In the first place, I will tell you about business affairs. When I wrote to you before, I told you William had sold his team, but the fall was so pleasant and hauling so high, he concluded to buy it back again. He

"Pick" Clark, Syrene's husband and a Confederate Soldier

Syrene Hughes Clark (photo by the well at her home in Alalbama that was mentioned in one of her letters

gave the same he sold it for, and the man allowed him $50 per thousand for hauling, so he made the same as he would have if he had not sold at all. Teaming has been much better this fall than in the summer.

We begin to think our luck has turned. The rent on our stable (we let a part of it) and the interest on the money we have let amounts to one hundred dollars per month. You may think it hardly possible, when you know how scarce money was when you left…. William has not got all his pay yet for hauling, so has about $250 due to him yet. He has let all his money for 6 and 8 per cent a month and has good security. I wish you and George were here, for I think you could do much better than you can there; but, of course, you must do as you think best…. I want you to discourage every one from coming here that you can, for the less teams the better.

Aurora
March 13[5]

I am tired to death this eve…. We have so many here on Sunday that it keeps me busy all day, but thank the Lord... dinner is over and dishes all done up and table set for morning.

We did feel some disappointed to hear you were not coming over here, but perhaps it is better for you not to come. Times look rather black here now, but we think they will be some better here in the summer. But it can't be very good unless we have snow or rain soon….

We think you will do well to come to Owens River. Everyone says it is a splendid farming country. There are quite a number going down from here to live…. when you get there, you can tell Miss Chandiler I would like to have her come over here, but she could not pay expenses dressmaking. There is quite a number [of dressmakers] here now, so that I can't get anything to do. If she has money to loan, she can do well on that. She can get from eight to ten percent a month and get as good security as she has in the place.

From your sister,
H.E. Hughes

Aurora
June 27, 1865

…. And now Bett, I suppose I can empathize with you, for I, too, am a widow for the time being. William has gone to California—started last Wednesday—is to be gone three or four weeks, and when he comes back, if he comes on horseback, he is going to see you. He has gone to see if he can get us a ranch, and if he does, we shall move over there as soon as he comes back; and if he does not buy one there, I think we shall go down Owens River way, for it is of no use for us to stay here.

There is nothing doing here. It is like Sunday here all the week. Lizzie [Harriet's sister] and I stay here all alone, sleep until ten in the morn so the day will not be so long—a privilege I suppose you can't have on account of the children.

You wanted to know if we ever heard from home. We have not had a letter since I can remember....

Mr. Hunewill was in last Friday and brought me two nice big fish. I wish you had been here to help us eat them, for I can tell you they were very nice, but we managed to give a part of them away, so they did not spoil. He says Esther and Frank are well. They are going to move on a ranch they own on the Meadows. I think he has given up making his "twenty five thousand, by *God*!"

I want you to write to me where George is and if he doesn't come home Saturday nights, and tell me how Bennie and Byron and Laura get along.... I was sorry to have you write that you were so lonesome, but we have to make the best of it. I hope we shall live near each other some time.

Harriet

Aurora
July 17 [probably 1865]

Well Bettie,

I am going to write you a few lines this eve, for I shall not get another chance until I get on the other side of the mountain. William has been home a week.... He did not get us a ranch, but business is very good there, and he is almost insane to get back. We are to start Monday, and I have worked myself almost to death to get ready.

We have four wild horses and a large load, and William thinks the road is too bad, so we can't go by the way of Silver Mountain [California]. I would like to see you all very much. I want you to write us and direct to Searsville.... We had a letter from Jane, which I will send to you. Give my love to George when you write to him and kiss the babies for me. How I would like to see them, and Bett, if you ever need a friend, you can depend on us. I feel bad to go over there and leave you here, but we can't do any thing here.... Will says, "Tell me of a better place and I will go there," but

Jane Hughes Powell, Bettie's sister and Crissie's aunt. I remember meeting aunt Jane

Syrene Hughes Clark, 1889, Uniontown, Alabama. Bettie's sister and Crissie's aunt

Bett, I don't know where we could find one.
>So good night,
>Hat Hughes

P.S. We have heard from both our brothers today. They are alive and well. Only think—been through three years of this [Civil] war and have not been wounded.

The Aurora exodus was underway. William and Harriet moved to Searsville, California. Meanwhile, some of Bettie's brothers and sisters were still living in Maine. This letter from Jane in 1865 recounted her health problems and the difficulties she faced as a single woman who had to work for a living. The letter may have been written to Esther and Napoleon, but letters were passed between the Hughes brothers and sisters, which may explain why Bettie kept this one.

Skowhegan, [Maine]
June 9, 1865

Dear Brother and Sister,

I must tell you what I have been trying to do. Thought I was smart enough to earn something this summer, for there were some things I must have this fall and winter—a dress and some winter underclothes, for I suffer so much with the cold. So went to work out in a family where the work was light and easy, but the first time I tried to wash, I strained the cords of my left hand so that I have not been able to work any with it for over a week....

I am at Mrs. Eddy's. Her health is not good, but I shall stop here this summer, if she can accommodate me.

I want to hear from you very much. When you write, direct to Skowhegan. All the folks are well at Madison.... heard from Syrene. She is in Alabama, married to a man by the [name] of Clark. John Hughes of Bath has been sick all last winter, has nearly lost the use of one of his eyes. I want to hear from Bettie very much.... Heard by the way that she has a pair of twins.

Rachel has gone up river to keep school. Sometimes I almost think I am forgotten; it is so long since I heard from you, and I do want to know where Bettie is.
>Write soon to your
>sister,
>M.J. Hughes

Rachel B. Hughes, Bettie's half sister and Crissie's aunt, a schoolteacher at Aurora and possibly Washoe City

Searsville, [California]
August 9, 1865[6]

Well Bettie,

 I suppose you are as mad as a March Hare, because we did not go and see you [on the trip from Aurora to California], but if ever I wanted to go anywhere in my life, it was to go and see you. But Bett, I can't always have my own way. William thought the road was bad, and the horses were wild and ugly, and he said it was no use in talking about it….

 Lizzie [her sister] and myself came from Folsom by the way of the cars and boat. It is a hard journey, and I never want to travel over the road again, but we got here all safe and have bought us a house…. two stories high and hard finished. It is a very good house. It has nine rooms and closets without number. It has five outside doors and nineteen in all. Lizzie and I have been striding the shortest cuts though the house since we came. Will is hauling lumber with five horses and has bought him a new wagon—paid $320. He makes a turn a day, gets home about five o'clock. I don't know but this is the best we could do.

 ….and now I must close soon for it is time to get supper for William, and I am tired. We have ironed today, and I have written, so Jane and I never worked so hard in my life as I have in the last four weeks…. Kiss the babies for me and give my love to George…. Now write and tell me how George is doing and when you are going to him, for I hate to think you are staying there alone.

      So no more at present,
      H. E. Hughes

Bridgeport,
April 13[7]

Sister Bet,

 I received your last [letter] some days ago and was very glad to hear from you and the family….

 I thought all winter that perhaps I could get over this spring and make a visit and bring Jane back, but find I am farther than ever from it. Hannah wrote me that she and Jane were coming. Now she writes that Hearne's brother is coming to visit them, and she can't come. I want to see all of you but can't come over. I want Jane to come over here, but I haven't the money to send her. We have been trying to sell, but no one wants to buy. We would be glad to leave here on Frank's account—no school within six miles…. Frank thinks he wants to go over there and see his cousins, but thinks if Ben was here they could go fishing and that would be better. And he wants to see his Aunt Jane—has heard so much about her and what a good cook she is—that is the most that interests him just now, is to get enough to eat.

Write as often as you can, and I will do the same. Excuse haste and mistakes.

From your sister,
Esther

Searsville
December 16, 1867

Dear Sister,

After so long a time, I have sat down to write you a line. This is the first time since I received your letter that I could answer it. Lizzie has been very sick. She had a nice little boy. It lived to be one month old and died. She has had the childbed fever, and she got better of that and now the dropsy has set in. We have Doctor Mollure to tend her....

I expected to hear you had an addition to your family when you wrote (you were so long about it) and was quite disappointed, but Lizzie says she hopes you will not have any more. I think she knows how to pity you.....[8]

You wanted me to send you some patterns, but I expect before this time you have it cut and made. I thought when I got your letter I would go to Mrs. Beans' and get some late patterns and send them to you, but I have not had an opportunity yet, but I will cut you the pattern of my dress skirt I had this fall and send it some time this week. They wear everything gored. You can cut waist and skirt together or separate. They cut them mostly plain waist and gored skirt like mine. I was down to San Jose this fall to Mrs. Chandlers. She says the large flowing sleeve is in fashion again, open to the arm size, but they are not worn around here yet. Lizzie and I sent to San Francisco and got us some hat frames and velvet and flowers and made us hats that are pretty, I think, and they only cost us three dollars apiece. Don't you think we are getting economical? Hard times have that about it, too.

And now I must close,
H E Hughes

By 1870, the Hughes brothers and sisters had all moved out West, with the exception of brother John. Rachel worked as a teacher at Aurora, and Jane stayed with family members. The letters show that money was still in short supply, and the family talked of the youngest sisters marrying rich men in order to make life easier.

Searsville
September 11, 1870
Sister Bettie,

Well, Bett, we got your letter all right... sorry to hear your health was so poor. I think you ought to have something strengthening to take and try and take care of yourself. Come over this fall and stop a while. It will do you good, and it won't cost you any more than it will to live there, if

George is away all the time… and I think Crissie would have a nice time in the rags, for Jane and I are making a rag carpet, and we have rags all over the house. And I have a little steer Bossie for Bennie, which shall be his own if he comes over. It is three weeks old tomorrow.

Well, Bettie, you complain of hard times, and I think it is the case almost everywhere, but we have no reason to complain. William has his same position he had last summer, and they hire his horses, too. I think you can do just as well over here as you can there, and only think how much better the climate is to live in. I wish you would coax George to take his team and move you over this fall. I think if he should get back here again, he would like it, and we could help one another and so get along first rate….

Now, I have something very serious to say to you and it is this: I want you to be careful that the Rev. Mr. Ricker does not seduce you, and tell George to keep a sharp lookout. No joking about this….

I had a letter from Esther not very long ago…. Well, I hope they will get rich. If they do, perhaps they might help you and me, if we should need it.

When R[achel] sent the paper, she wrote that her school would close in a week. Perhaps she and the doctor are married…. I think if she gets the doctor, she will get a good husband. If he is a little older, that won't hurt her….

          Harriet

East Madison, Maine
September 2, 1871

Dear Girls:

Well, I hardly know what time I will start, but think, in all probability, in about a month. If I go by rail, will stop at Washoe till Napoleon Bonaparte comes after me, so make ready to go over with me and spend the winter. Esther will be ever so glad to have you, for she doesn't consider me anything more than blood relation….

Well, you must excuse a short letter this time, as I'm coming so soon. I will get your teaspoons, if my means holds out, which I fear they will not. Small teaspoons are $7.50 to $10.00 per half dozen; larger spoons, $7.00 to $8.00 per pair, so you see silver is pretty well high, but I'll do the best I can for you….

        From your maiden
        sister, Rac

Rachel B. Hughes, Bettie's half sister and Crissie's aunt, a schoolteacher at Aurora and possibly Washoe City

Geoffrey's Cove
August 28, 1878

Dear Bettie,

.... We were sorry to hear Ben was sick. Hope he is well before this. And to tell you what I think about you being so miserable? I just think it is hard work, and I don't believe there is any need of it, now that you have a good home. Just make up your mind as I have, that we have done hard work enough. I don't expect to carry anything out of this world, and I am sure I don't care to leave much for our friends to quarrel over, and I am just going to take all the comfort I can....

       H. E. Hughes

Bridgeport
May 8, 1880

Dear Betty,

....The house is not finished yet, but we hope to get moved this week. Esther is very impatient.... Have not seen Hannah yet, but we may go over [to Bodie] today....

I am going to send you a nice apron pattern, and in the blanket the piece pinned on is like the dress Esther had made for herself. My trunk was delayed a week, so I wore her dress and kept it. It is trimmed with turkey red and is very becoming. Your gloves I will keep and will send you some money today, $5.00 by express. I would like to know where to send for the book you take. Please send their address, also the address of Butterick's if you can find it.... I saw one of Butterick's books in Carson and liked it very much. It is $100 a year.

I want very much to hear how you are getting along. Don't be envious of Esther having a new house. She doesn't take any more comfort than you do. Are the children going to school? Write soon, and Crissie must write some, too, for she will tell me all the extra news. It is very cold and backward here, and from nine to thirteen in a family.

       In haste from
       M.J. Hughes

Searsville, California
December 1, 1882

Dear Betts & all the rest,

Well, the news is Mr. Hunewill has made us a visit, a short one. He and Frank came New Year's Day. Only stayed one night was all. We were real glad to see him. He looks like a little lord and feels as well as two, he says. He has lost fifty thousand dollars, and I should judge he had plenty left by the appearance. Says he and Frank has spent six hundred in the city since he came down, I think he said. He (or they) had been out to the Ocean House aught times, and I think if Frank wanted to go to any other place, the old man would take him there ... Don't let George see this, but as I can't see you, I must write it. Anything Frank says or does is all right with him. He has taken him from school—says his eyes are so weak, he can't study any more. He was under treatment for them. Said he should like to have made a lawyer out of him, but should have to give it up. Thought he would let him take charge of the ranch, as the old man has so much business, he can't attend to it. Suppose he thought if Frank were a lawyer, it would give him plenty of employment attending to his business, as he says he has lawsuits on hand all the time.

I said, "Hunewill, why don't you come on this side of the mountain and live where you can have some pleasure?"

He said, "I could not make spending money here. I spend an awful sight of money," and I guess he does. Think it is well they have the ranch to fall back on. He says his sawmills are not worth anything now that the railroads go to Mono Lake.

I have been making rugs... going to draw one more, and then am going to braid the rest of my rags. I have got lots of them, and you know it takes one a long time to make so many rugs, but my time is much like a setting hen's—don't amount to much....

Lizzie and Peers has gone to the city today to celebrate their crystal wedding, been married fifteen years today. It does not seem possible it is so long. William and I have been married twenty-five years last September, but we didn't have a silver wedding, as we thought silver was too scarce. Give our love to all.

From your sister,
H. E. Hughes

Searsville, California
January 22, 1883
Dear Bett,

Your letters and Crissie's have all been received.... Don't worry over that little money you owe us. You can have your whole lifetime to pay it, but appears you want to get it paid, and I don't blame you for that. We shall never distress you for it, so don't worry. Think we all will have enough to carry us through, and that is all we can want, as we can't take anything with us.[9]

Searsville, California
March 30, 1890, Sunday

William has written to George, but I think the letter would not be complete unless I put in my little say. We are all well. William and [daughter] Minnie have gone out in the pasture to see how the colts are getting along, and I

Minerva Hughes, Crissie's cousin and dear friend, the adopted daughter of William and Harriet Hughes

Alex and Lizzie Peers, Harriet Hughes's sister

guess they'll get a good wetting. It was just lovely when they started, but it is raining hard now.... Minnie gets along very well with her music.... She has played all this term the marches for the school. She can play thirteen pieces besides the exercises.... I am glad you are having such good times sleigh riding with your furs and rocks. Don't think I envy you one bit. Wish you had the furs long ago. They have been laying in the house for years doing no one any good. You or Lizzie could share with me the last dollar I had, and I would be just as pleased to have you or her have everything nice and good, as I would to have it myself, and I believe you both feel the same toward me.

Tell Ben when his school finishes in May to come down here and make us a visit. I want Crissie to come when we get moved and stay all winter.

Love to Jane and all.
Harriet

CHAPTER FOUR
Crissie

CHILDHOOD, 1866-1876

CHRISTINE HARRIET ANDREWS was born at 6:16 a.m. on September 6, 1866 at the Andrews's home in Washoe City. Crissie was a welcomed child. She brought joy to George and Bettie Andrews, the grieving parents whose twins had died just one year earlier. Bettie—her adventurous spirit rocked off its foundation and her health compromised—now refused further adventure or even a move from Washoe City unless George promised stability.

Crissie entered a noisy world in Washoe Valley. Fifteen steam-powered sawmills processed lumber for the Comstock. Freight wagons, like the one George Andrews operated, rumbled through the streets on the way to Virginia City hauling timber to shore up the mines, lath and shingles to build homes and businesses, and cordwood to power the ore mills. Washoe City's population grew from 200 to 1,005, according to 1860 and 1861 censuses. Nearby, the small towns of Ophir, Franktown, and Galena were also prosperous.[1]

Crissie's childhood was spent at Washoe City with her parents and older brother Ben. Her education began there, probably at the elementary school, although her father was a schoolteacher before coming west and probably provided some lessons at home, especially penmanship.

Crissie told me her favorite playmate at Washoe City was Persia Bowers, daughter of Eilley Orrum and Sandy Bowers, whose fortune came from the Comstock. Crissie was one of the children invited to play at the Bowers' Mansion, and she remembered those times with Persia as carefree times of make-believe and adventure, even when she fell into their pool several times.

Crissie spent many happy hours romping through the grounds and playing in the [Bowers'] house. The one thing [that] impressed her childish mind most was the cupola.... she and Persia made that a favorite retreat, climbing the stairs that were in it and feeling far away from the outer world, although few restrictions were placed on their activity in any rooms.... Mrs. Bowers was kind to the children and often expressed a wish for a way to keep record of their play with pictures.... When the children tired of their watchtower in the cupola they dangled their feet in the water and as a special treat were permit-

Crissie Andrews, 1868, 2 years old

Crissie at 3 years, 5 months

ted to visit the green houses....

Those happy days playing with Persia were short-lived. After Sandy Bowers's death, Eilley turned the mansion into an historical site and resort. Persia was sent to take music lessons and boarded with friends in Reno. Each week, Persia traveled home to visit her mother by train. Following a visit in July 1874, Persia sickened and died. Crissie lost her playmate when Persia was just 12 years old. Persia was buried next to her father in the family plot near the mansion.[4]

By the time Crissie was three years old, great changes were taking place in beautiful Washoe Valley. Lumber mills were built nearer to the Comstock mines in order to reduce overhead, but it also reduced the demand for hauling services like her father's. Added to that, the demand for timber dwindled right along with the rich ores in the Virginia City mines. Then, the Virginia-Carson Railroad was completed in 1869, and the Central Pacific Railroad was destined to follow the Truckee River—both railroads routed commerce away from Washoe City.[5]

Reno's future now shone brighter than Washoe City's. In 1872, when Crissie was six years old, the county seat was moved from Washoe City to Reno.[6] The time had come for Bettie and George to establish a more dependable income. Through a combination of family's savings and trade for his work on the irrigation ditches, George acquired a few hundred acres west of Reno.

Crissie was 8 years old on May 16, 1874 (according to Crissie's diary) when George moved his family to the Andrews Ranch and began growing hay. Alfalfa was introduced to the area in 1863 and quickly became the cash crop for Washoe County ranches. Some fields yielded two or three crops a year "amounting to six to eight tons per acre."[7]

George built a small, wood-frame house near what is now the intersection of Plumb Lane and South McCarran Boulevard.[7] There, George's sister, Crissie's Aunt Martha, joined them for Thanksgiving in 1875. Forty years later, she wrote about the first Thanksgiving celebrated at the ranch and remembered that Bettie sold eggs for 75 cents per dozen.

Antrim, N.H.
October 25, 1915

[Part of a letter to Syrene, Crissie's daughter]
.... I was the last person at home [in New Hampshire, when George left for the West] to take his hand and the first and only one of the family to meet him "beyond the Rockies." I shall not forget his look when I told him goodbye, when he left us in the train going to Elko.... He was living

where you do now, and while we were there, gave up his bed and slept in the unfinished chamber upon sheepskins on the floor! Aunt Jane was there, too, and we had Thanksgiving dinner together, the first for 18 years. We ate in one end of the kitchen. I remember they were digging a well out back of the house, and I heard him say he was afraid to go deeper because the water might be warm....

Your loving,
Aunt Martha

Back in New Hampshire, that same Thanksgiving, George's parents died without having seen their son again. Aunt Martha's letters never mentioned the cause of their death, but the fact that they died just two days apart makes me wonder. Could they have died of food poisoning from a holiday meal or perhaps an illness such as cholera? After their parents died, Aunt Martha pleaded with her brother, asking George to return to New Hampshire and settle his parents' estate.

Nevada, Missouri
November 13, 1879

Dear George,
   As the anniversary of the death of our parents approaches, my thoughts instinctively turn to our old home and our family connections.... there were four generations at one time in the house. Grandfather French would be proud of them! When I think how we have been neglecting his grave, I think we are making a poor return for what he gave all of us—though you knew *you* had the "biggest *slice*."
   What will people say of us? That we are all reduced to poverty or are "no account?" Would grandfather desire us to do as we have done, and should we thus neglect the grave of our own parents? You are so far off that you cannot realize the importance of attending to it, and your attention is required at your own home.

Sister Martha

Aunt Martha Byers and her family lived at Elko, Nevada, for two years. Her husband served as minister, and she said, "We left the church eight times as large as we found it and the Sunday school in running order." Aunt Martha's letters contain historical facts, such as the price of produce, along with her opinions on politics, opposition to war, and advice on child rearing (May 30, 1878). Aunt Martha opposed war and supported women's suffrage. In a 1915 letter, she told Crissie "Your Great Great Aunt Mercy French, born in the 18th century, was a suffragist—a spin-

Crissie Andrews

Crissie, 16, c. 1882

ster of the olden type. A hundred years ago, she wrote the paper petitioning the New Hampshire legislature for the right of our sex to vote."

Crissie Andrews to Cousin Minnie, 1888

Elko, Nevada
October 18, 1876
My Dear Brother and Family,
   Today, we received the box of tomatoes and honey, and it is truly a rich treat.... We judge there were seventy pounds, which would have cost us $7.00 in Elko. When I wrote I said I would buy, but you sent no bill. We have been buying peaches and apples from Utah and get them for about one-half the retail price in Elko....
   Thanksgiving will soon be here. Can't you all come to Elko and spend a little time with us? Come one, come all. We will do the best we can for you, but I don't know whether we can have the pumpkin pies....
                                       Martha

In later years, Crissie sent apples from the Andrews Ranch to New Hampshire, and Aunt Martha commented, "... what makes me doubly appreciative is the fact that my brother set out the trees. He must have had some good in his heart to want to do such work."

While Aunt Martha continued writing letters to George and Bettie, she also started writing to Crissie. Early in their correspondence, the bond between Aunt Martha and Crissie was sealed. "I think Crissie beats her father at writing letters, for she gives me more news, and when she gets a better hand, she will be a nice writer. Keep on, Crissie, and don't wait for me to answer. Your letters are always welcome."

TEENAGE YEARS, 1876-1880

Crissie spent her teen years at the Andrews Ranch west of Reno. Now that her father could spend evenings at home with the family, he seldom did. Often he went to his favorite saloon, Thyes and Reese on Second Street between Virginia Street and Sierra Street, and just as often Crissie was sent to bring him home. Instead of being a traumatized "child of an alcoholic" by today's standards, Crissie remembered those evenings as fun. She and her father rode home in the buggy on the country road and sang songs all the way.

Ben Andrews

Ben and Crissie did chores and helped their parents, but once the work was done, Crissie loved to ride her horse across the wide-open spaces. She would often go to play with neighbor children. Their nearest neighbors, the Schiappacasse (pronounced Shep-case), were a half-mile away and kitty-corner across the street from the present location of the Ranch House

As she matured, Crissie was enrolled in one of the first classes at the Bishop Whitaker School for Girls. Boasting an education similar to finishing schools in the East, the school opened in 1876 and offered the equivalent of today's high school diploma. After four years at Whitaker's, students were qualified to enter college.

WHITAKER SCHOOL FOR GIRLS, RENO

This school for girls was founded… by the Right Rev. O.W. (Ozi William) Whitaker, D.D., (Episcopal) Bishop of Nevada from 1869 to 1886. It was established to give the girls of Nevada the opportunity of obtaining within their own State a thorough education, in a well-guarded *Christian Home*, where they would be surrounded by good influences, and be cared for as daughters in the family as to their health, manners and character. The aim of the school is to develop the pupils into refined, cultured, Christian women, well fitted for all the duties of practical and social life, and trained up to be all that daughters, wives and mothers ought to be. The object of the discipline of the school is to instill just principles of action, to cultivate a love for the right, and to teach girls that "greatest of all human achievements" – self-government…. Music, drawing, painting, French, and German are taught by experienced and accomplished teachers. The school… has a good gymnasium, library, chemical apparatus, cabinet of minerals, etc…. Pupils taking the full work of the academic course will be prepared for admission to any college. Such pupils will be admitted to the Stanford University upon certificate from Whitaker School, and no further examination will be required. [Day students paid $6 a month compared to $30 for boarding students. Lessons in piano, singing, French, German, drawing, and painting cost extra.] [8]

…. Six and one-half acres of ground in the northwest portion of the town were secured and building was commenced June 1, 1876…. The school was duly opened with forty scholars with Miss Kate Sill, Principal, and four assistants. [9]

Regular exercises in reading, writing, spelling, defining, and composition, are continued through the course. Especial attention is given to English composition and the formation of a correct taste in reading.[10]

Ben and Crissie Andrews

"Reno 50 years ago," c. 1887 from Fred Stradmuller

Donner Lake and tummy ache, c. 1887, Crissie sitting front center on a picnic with friends

Camp Reno, Crissie lying down in front

Camp Reno, Crissie on left standing

Crissie's graduating class, June 10, 1890
(Crissie on left)

Morrill Hall, University of Nevada c. 1889

The school closed in 1894....The trees and grounds have been preserved as Whitaker Park at 9th Street between Washington and Ralston Streets in Reno.[11]

Crissie loved music, and her lovely singing voice and talent for whistling were in demand. Letters from the aunts mentioned Crissie's musical talents, comments that were mixed with opinions on prohibition, warnings about the grasshopper infestation, and concern for Bettie's continued poor health. The Bridgeport and Bodie aunts reported tough economic times, scarlet fever, and a fire at Bodie.

Lawrence, Kansas
May 10, 1881

My Dear Crissie;
    I can hardly realize that you are the little girl that used to play the organ on the chairs when I first knew you.... I am glad to know of your mother's good health and that your Aunt Jane is with you. Does she never talk of taking a trip east? I think you will all feel like it, if the grasshoppers give you a good visit. I hope they will not eat the land up. People here are just getting over the effects of the grasshopper season in Kansas. Everything looks prosperous now... and best of all our Prohibition law works well so far. Some are complaining that "moneyed men" are leaving; but who are they? Whiskey dealers and whiskey lovers. Who take their places? Anti-whiskey men and religious people who wish to raise their families where the bane of our country is not found....

                      Write soon,
                      M.J. Byers

Bridgeport
August 12, 1892

Dear Crissie,
    When your letter came, I intended to answer right away, but before I could get about it, the children, Millie and Stanley, were taken down with the scarlet fever, and then we had no time and were afraid of sending the fever to you. The fact of your having had it once doesn't count. Lots of people here have had it twice and some three times. Lucile didn't have it at all, and she was right with the others and helped to take care of them. I will put camphor on this, but I don't think there is any danger, but burn it up all the same....

Christine H. Andrews, June 12, 1890, graduation from University of Nevada. Morrill Hall in background. Painting from photograph by Shiela Lonie. Wood for frame came from Crissie's chicken shack.

I suppose you heard that Bodie was nearly wiped out. It was about like the Reno fires. Rachel said the air was full of burning shingles and stuff, and she had no one to help her, but not a spark fell on any of her buildings. Johnny [Hannah Hughes Hearnes's son] is here working in haying....

We began haying the 20th of July and will finish in about eight or nine weeks. I have a Chinaman, but he told me yesterday that he was tired and wanted to leave. We have over twenty in the family. Alice and I are just as busy as we can be. We pick and put up currants and gooseberries all day and then sew all night, but tonight we made a change and write.. Of course, you have finished haying.... How are your Mother and Jane and everybody else? And how is Ben? Is he married yet?...

From your
Aunt Esther

To Crissie from teacher Wm. B. Daugherty, May 1890

"The weary teacher sat alone while twilight gathered on; and not a sound was heard around, the boys and girls were gone. In sad soliloquy of no avail is constant zeal life's sacrifice is loss, the hopes of morn so golden turn each evening into dross."

Crissie Andrews

Bodie, Mono County, California
December 18, 1883

Dear Crissie;
    I expect you all think I have been waiting for postage to lower a little, but when I tell you that I have had from eight to twelve in family for nearly two years, you will know I have not had much time to write.
    I have a cook just now who was here several weeks as a patient but it will not last long with no pay.
    Times are very dull here, but still there seems to be more Christmas toys and traps than I have ever seen here before. I have got Johnny a velocipede stowed away upstairs. There will be a Christmas tree in the church or Hall. Bodie supports two churches now....
    The papers are full of murders. I dread to look in a paper, for I get so nervous when I am alone. The patients, with the exception of three, sleep upstairs. The others occupy the front room where Jane and I took down the partition, so I lock the middle door, which leaves Johnny and I alone after dark.... Please write soon...
                  Your
                    Aunt Hannah

CRISSIE'S SECRET, 1885 - 1886

Crissie grew into a lively young woman, who loved to sing and dance and spend time with her friends. From the time she was 13, the aunts expressed concern for Crissie's safety. Aunt Esther Hunewill gathered her courage and spoke directly to the point.

Bridgeport, California
April 24, 1880

Well, Bettie,
Jane has written everything, but I had something to say myself, and I suppose you will be mad about it, too, but I can't help it. Hannah has just sent me word that Nellie French, that little girl that used to stay with her in Silver [Mountain City], had a baby and that made me think of Crissie. I felt so afraid that you would let her out of your sight. I told Jane to put in a word in her letter, but she said she would not, so thought I would do it myself. She is the only girl in the Hughes family, and it would kill us all if any thing happened to her, and you can't be too careful. Perhaps you think it isn't any of my business.
                  Goodbye,
                  Esther Hunewill

In spite of warnings, Crissie did attend dances without a personal chaperone. Crissie and her mother were friends with Alfred and Mary Doten and Mary's daughter, Millie Stoddard, of Virginia City. Doten kept a daily journal from 1849 to 1903, and it contains brief notations about one of Crissie's social activity that led to trouble. On November 26, 1885, following Thanksgiving dinner, Doten wrote, "Millie and Miss Crissie Andrews went with a young fellow to a grand masquerade ball."[12]

In later years, Crissie never spoke of the events that followed, which means details are sketchy, but just four months after the dance, at age 19, Crissie married George H. Brown. Her secret might have remained buried in county records, but many years later I found a tiny newspaper clipping at the ranch house—an obituary for Crissie's baby—a baby none of us knew existed. Even then, Crissie refused to tell me about it, but I never forgot. I uncovered her long-held secret just a few years ago, locked away in old newspaper accounts and court documents. First came the announcement of her marriage:

THE ALTAR
Brown – Andrews – On Truckee Meadows near Reno, by the Rev. G.M. Spencer, George H. Brown to Miss Crissie Andrews. (*Reno Evening Gazette*, March 9, 1886)

Then, just four months after their wedding, Brown was arrested and charged with theft on two occasions. Eventually, he was sent to the state prison.

> George Brown, the fellow who on Saturday [July 10, 1886] finished a fifty day's sentence for stealing a suit of clothes in Wadsworth, was again arrested yesterday morning for burglarizing C.J. Brooklins' store. As several of the coins found on him can be sworn to by more than one witness, Mr. Brown's chances for a stone-cutting job with Warden Bell are regarded as good! (*Reno Evening Gazette*, Monday, July 12, 1886)

> George H. Brown, who burglarized C.J. Brooklins' store, had his preliminary hearing before Justice Young this morning, and was held to answer in the sum of $1,000. In deficit of bail he was committed. (*Reno Evening Gazette*, Tuesday, July 13, 1886)

Crissie filed for and was granted a divorce in October 1886. The handwritten court document tells the story.

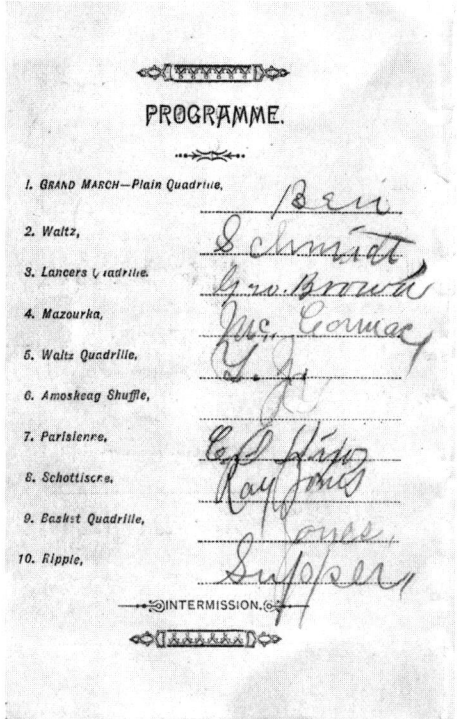

Dance card for the Grand Uniform Ball of the Reno Hose Co., No. 1. When Crissie danced with George Brown, her soon-to-be husband

Crissie Andrews wearing gold beads that were passed down from Aunt Harriet to Crissie, then to me.

FINDING THE FACTS

That the Defendant George H. Brown and the Plaintiff Crissie Andrews, now Brown, were united in marriage March 8th, 1886 at the County of Washoe, State of Nevada....

That the defendant at that time or about May 10, 1886, departed without the knowledge of plaintiff for San Francisco in the state of California and there remained till on or about the 21st day of May aforesaid.

That upon his return from San Francisco, he went to the town of Wadsworth... and committed Petty Larceny and was therefore... committed to the Common jail of said County of Washoe for a term of fifty days.

That said action was commenced on the 7th day of July by filing a complaint and serving Summons in said action while the defendant was in the common jail of said County, charging the Defendant with "extreme cruelty."

That since said action was served on the defendant in the County of Washoe said State of Nevada on the 10th day of July 1886 after his discharge from prison.

That he made default in said action,

That the Plaintiff suffered in mind and in body from and because of the course of conduct of the Defendant toward her, that he was convicted of theft, committed to said County and placed in the Common jail for said offense.

That after said conviction of said crime of Petty Larceny and after his discharge from jail, the defendant committed at Reno in said county the crime of burglary, and was therefore duly convicted in said court thereof upon a vote of a jury and was duly sentenced to the State Prison for a time of four years, where the Defendant now is.

That said crime of Burglary aggravated and continued the condition of mind and body of the Plaintiff and caused her Great Pain – That the Defendant showed he was abandoned and utterly regardless of the feelings of the Plaintiff and had no regard for his wife or relation of husband.

That the condition of health of the Plaintiff would continue so long as she would be or continue to be the wife of Defendant.

Crissie Brown vs. George H. Brown

The above entitled cause having come up for hearing on the 2nd day of October, A.D. 1886 in open court at the hour of One O'clock P.M. of said day... the Plaintiff appeared by her attorney Wm. Webster Esq. an attorney of said court.... It is ordered, adjudged and decreed by the Court that the marriage relation now and heretofore existing between the Plaintiff in this, Crissie Brown, and the Defendant, the said George H. Brown, and the relation of husband and wife now and heretofore existing between said Plaintiff and Defendant is set aside and declared to be no longer...

And it is further ordered adjudged and decreed that the said Plaintiff ... shall be known by and have the full right to use her said maiden name of Crissie Andrew.

The fact that Crissie never mentioned the marriage or her baby told me that she felt the divorce was scandalous and scarred her reputation. Also, 1886 was still a time when women did not talk publicly about pregnancy. Among her collection of letters, a woman might obliquely refer to childbirth as "being sick," followed by, "and I got myself a baby girl." Thus, Crissie chose to bear the burden of her sad and painful mistake alone.

The next information I have about my grandmother is that Crissie enrolled at the Nevada State University in 1888. I can only guess that the two years after the death of her baby and her divorce were filled with pain. However, Crissie's determination was unbreakable and adversity only made her stronger.

UNIVERSITY DAYS, 1888-1890

In 1888, both Crissie and her beloved older brother Ben enrolled in the business department of the Nevada State University located in Reno.

Crissie left, graduate of the University of Nevada 1890

> "The course of study in this department is designed to prepare young men and women for entrance upon a practical business life. It is not encumbered with any superfluous studies and deals with the practical requirements of a business education."[13]

Learning bookkeeping and business transactions was necessary if either of the Andrews children planned to operate the ranch after their parents died.

> "...Le Roy Brown was elected President [1887].... Miss H.K. Clapp was placed in charge of the business department.... W. B. Daugherty was made Master of Bookkeeping in 1888.... This (Morrill Hall) is located in the middle of the campus. In it are the President's office, the faculty room, registrar's office and the physics and chemistry recitation room on the first floor.... In the basement is the library. (The University also had the Experiment Station, Mining Building, Stewart Hall, Gymnasium, and Lincoln Hall.)
> The Commercial School is designed to meet the demands of a short business course. The studies required are bookkeeping, penmanship, typewriting and shorthand, and

telegraphy. [Social life for students consisted of literary societies and social clubs. Dances were held frequently, and athletics clubs were also popular.]¹⁴

Crissie was 22 when she enrolled in college, and at the same time, she returned to Reno's social scene. She sang in the university chorus for the play "Ramona," a play that was presented at McKissick's Opera House.

McKissick Opera House where Crissie and Ben sang

> PROGRAM GIVES NAMES OF EARLY DAY ACTORS HERE
> From a time worn theater program, part of which is missing.... "Head Shepherd of the Rancho" was the part Judge Norcross [Federal Judge Frank H. Norcross] played in "Ramona" presented by a group of Reno players to dedicate the McKissick's Opera House on June 13 and 14, 1888 the program discloses.
> In the chorus were Misses Crissie Andrews, Lizzie Kinkead, Ada Finlayson, Flora Pinniger, Kittie Loomis, Cora Fergason and the following men whose initials of their first names were not given: Messrs. Schmidt, Mulbach, Penniger, Beebe, Andrews, Cook, McNeely, Holesworth and Roff....¹⁵

In May 1889, Doten recorded in his diary"... wife was at ball at Nevada Theater, given by the young gents and ladies of the State University. She went with Chrissie [sic] Andrews." Then for the Fourth of July celebration, "Mrs. Andrews and daughter Crissy [sic] and Mrs. Powell dined with us—Evening fireworks in public square, front of theater—McKissick's Opera House."¹⁶

After that first year at college, Ben transferred to Napa College in California, where he pursued studies in acting and debate. Meanwhile, Crissie earned her business degree and graduated in 1890. At her graduation ceremony, Crissie was scheduled to read an essay, along with other members of her class. However, a newspaper article noted that she did not attend, but I don't know her reason. Crissie always seemed proud of graduating from the university. Also, although it was exceptional for that time, she told me her mother and father valued an equal education for Crissie and her brother.

CHAPTER FIVE
Crissie Faces Death and Divorce

WHEN MY FIRST HUSBAND, Bob Scharbach was sent to the Korean conflict, I had a brand new baby girl and nowhere to turn, except to Grandma Crissie and the ranch. The only thing Crissie said when we arrived was, "Isn't it nice to have the ranch to come home to?"

As I have discovered all the pieces of my grandmother's life, I realize it was a rhetorical question. How often, and through so many difficult times, the ranch must have been a haven for her.

Crissie graduated from college in 1890 at the age of 23, well schooled in the social graces from attending Reno's Whitaker School for Girls, but already a divorced woman. She was probably not on the list of Reno's proper and marriageable young ladies. Whatever hopes, dreams, and plans she held in her heart, the events of the next five years changed Crissie and shaped her destiny.

BROTHER BENJAMIN

One of Crissie's dearest friends was her only brother Benjamin. Her mother Bettie described Benjamin in her letters as a happy-go-lucky child. The letters from Benjamin to his mother and Crissie were from a young man, who was full of life and promise.

Among Grandma Crissie's letters were several from Benjamin's high school teacher, Orvis Ring.[1] At the time he wrote in the early 1880s, Ring was teaching school in Winnemucca. He commented on a few of Ben's friends who were getting into mischief. Among the names Ring mentioned were Charlie Eaton, Marcus Frederick, Charlie McK., George McF., and George Laughton. He also invited several of his former students to visit him in Winnemucca, including Ben.

> I still live in the parsonage all alone. I eat at the restaurant. Come and stay with me a week or more…. Well, how do you get along at school? What are you studying? Have you got whipped yet?
>
> I am sorry Geo. McF. had trouble. I wish he were out here with me. I think I could get along with him! If I only had a small home furnished, I

would keep back [save money] and send for Geo. to come and live with me. Would you not come also? I hear from Charlie Eaton every week. He does not have much time for foolishness. I think he has to study *pretty hard.* (September 27, 1882)

Benjamin's friends were not the only ones stirring up trouble. Ring mentioned that Crissie's also had conflicts with some of her high school teachers. Ben was three years older than Crissie and may have been in college at the time of the Ring letters. However, in 1888, Crissie and Ben both were registered at the Nevada State University. Crissie would have been 22 and Ben was 25. Crissie's marriage and divorce accounted for her late start at the university. Perhaps Ben's college education was delayed because he was needed to help on the ranch. In addition, the Andrews were not wealthy, so I don't know how much money was available for college.

Benjamin and Crissie had a great affection for each other, which was revealed in the older brother's gentle teasing. When Ben transferred to Napa College in California, he wrote a series of letters addressed to "my dear sister Christopher." Those were letters Crissie cherished for decades, and she always had "Uncle Ben's picture" hanging on the wall at the ranch. I now realize that his letters, and those of others, hinted at a serious problem back at the ranch.

Ben Andrews, 1888, while attending Napa College

Napa, California
Aug. 5, 1889

Dear Sister,
  Your kind and welcome letter came at hand today. I was very glad to hear from home. I have not felt homesick as yet; the faculty makes it a specialty to make everything as homelike as they can. It is just delightful here…. There are lots of nice young ladies here. We are supposed to go [to] church twice on Sunday.
  Charlie and I are rooming together. I find him a very genial sort of fellow. There are fourteen or somewhere in that neighborhood from Nevada. We are all acquainted and have good times… I am glad to know Pa is doing so well.
       Benjamin H.
       Andrews

Napa, California
Sep. 6, 1889

My Dear Sister Christopher,
  I received a short letter from you saying you had been

around with the butter for Pap. I am glad you are having so many picnics. You must still be in town yet.... That harmonica quartet must have been grand as rendered. How are the University Cadets getting along with drill? They must be... so they can handle a musket quite well.

Napa College
October 20, 1889

Dear Mama,

How is Papa? I received your last letter and am always glad to hear from home. If I do not get a letter when I think one due, it gives me an uneasy feeling, and I begin to think that everything is not all right.

I have estimated the hay and will place the figures below on the same paper. If you have given me the right figures, I think I got the right amounts... I think the first crop of hay turned out quite well. If the second did as well, considering, you must have about five hundred tons. You did not send me the measurement of both ends, so I do not know what the average is. In measuring a stack of hay, it is necessary to measure both ends, find the sum, add them together, and take ½ of the sum, which will be the average width.

I still remain your
affectionate,
Son Benjamin

Napa City, California
November 16, 1889

My Dear Little Sister Christopher,

It seems to me like a coon's age since I received a letter from you. I received an invitation to go to a dance given by the Nevada State University Athletic Society November 29. Sorry that I cannot be there. If you go, dance once for me.

Grace Griswold is married. I received her wedding card. It was sent from Eureka, California. She married a Mr. Fenton. She is the second one of the merry fourteen to get married....

It will soon be time for me to come home; now only one more month after this. I am out for a debate in the society. Are you still going to school? I suppose everything is quiet at the University by this time. I have nearly completed the arithmetic and commercial law, but have not got along so fast in bookkeeping as some of the rest. I have not wasted any time since I have been here. From what Ma says, I will not return again next session....

From Your Loving
Brother, Benjamin

Orvis Ring, one of Ben's teachers. Ring went on to become the Superintendent of Public Instruction from 1891-1895 and 1899-1910, according to Alf Doten diary, pp. 40 and 41.

Bettie Hughes Andrews

George W. Andrews, 1873

The question, "How is Papa?" was more than a courtesy. At some point, Crissie's father began drinking heavily, and by 1889, George's drinking obviously affected his ability to run the ranch. Bettie sought her son's help in calculating the yield of the hay crop (even though Ben struggled with bookkeeping), while Crissie delivered butter to customers in town. In fact, Crissie may have been staying with another family in Reno to be nearer the university and protected from the problems at home. However, Crissie and Ben were steadily pulled into the rift between their parents.

BETTIE AND GEORGE DIVORCE

Bettie became desperate. She pleaded for help from her family, and although the letter containing Bettie's plea is long gone, the reply from her brother's wife Harriet speaks volumes about the extent of the Andrews's problems. Apparently, William and Harriet did not go to Reno as asked, but instead extended financial help and a visit to California for Bettie.

Searsville, California
April 27, 1890

Dear Bettie,
 Your letter came all safe. We were glad to hear from you, but sorry to hear of your trouble. Keep up good courage and try to think everything is for the best…. I don't think it is hardly possible for William to go over there. It will take all his time in Redwood for several weeks…. he is *head over heels in business* this year.
 He has written to George today and sent him a note to sign. He did not say anything to him about you signing it, but will send it to you to sign afterwards. He asked him to send him some money, if he could. Don't think he could take any offence at anything he wrote.
 I want you to send me Ben's address. I want to write him to come down here before he goes home….
 Love to all and a large share for yourself.
                                From sister,
                                Harriet

While Bettie took a much-needed break in California, Ben was in charge of the ranch, and Crissie returned home to help. I found the clearest reference to George's problem with alcohol in the postscript that Bettie wrote from California.

Searsville, San Mateo, California
February 6, 1889

My Dear Children,

I am glad you are getting a long so well, but I am sorry Pa was disappointed about his letter, as I wrote him from the city as soon as I arrived and asked him to come down. It was nice to sell the pigs, but I am surprised at Ben wanting to spend it for such trash. He's no baby and would run a ranch into the ground at that rate. Don't do it. It won't burn your pocket. Try it.

It seems like I have been gone a long time. Mr. H. is here, and he seemed quite smart when he came out, but his medicine is all gone and he is not so well. He hasn't drank any liquor since he came down, as his medicine will not admit of it.

We have been to the Palo Alto Ranch and the Stanford University, which is just well begun.[2]

I thought your white skirt was on that trunk with the shirts. If it is not, I can't tell you where it is. The tongues were not cooked. I told you, they are in the south kitchen by the stove in a can....

From your
Dear Mother,
Write, both of you.
Mrs. Geo. W.
Andrews

George Andrews favorite saloon, Thyes and Reese Crystal Saloon, located between Virginia and Sierra Streets in Reno

P.S. If Pa wants to come down, help him all you can. It will do him good. Ma. [Response to an item in the *Reno Gazette*.]

...every good citizen should be willing to assist in such an enterprise, but how would it do to close those saloons by law, and let the fathers—that are spending their time and money drinking—build better and more attractive homes and set a better example for the boys? Who would be more willing than those same boys and girls to help make pleasant homes.... Thanks to the Gazette, it advocates true principles.

Interior of the Thyes and Reese Crystal Saloon

Searsville, California
February 8, 1889

My dear,

I wrote you all yesterday but Aunt Esther is writing, so will I. She is going to the City Saturday the 9th, and possibly will go up before I do, as I shall wait for an answer to Harriet's and my letter before I go. I think it would do Pa good to see the old places (if he would leave his bottle home).... the cold doesn't trouble me now, but it is very warm for the season....

Mother,
Betsy G. Andrews

George's drinking became intolerable. In 1892, Bettie filed for divorce and charged him with drunkenness, abusive language, and adultery. The court found in her favor on all charges except adultery. Bettie kept the ranch and all the personal property. She paid George $2,000, and he took two colts of his choice. Forty acres west of Reno went to Crissie, while Benjamin was not mentioned in the final property settlement.

ANDREWS DIVORCE DECREE

The following excerpts are from the Andrews's divorce decree, which is on file at the Washoe County Clerk's office in Reno. The document is packed with information, such as the date of the couple's marriage and how long they resided in Nevada prior to their divorce, that verified important dates in my great grandmother's life. I was also interested to read the list of personal property they had acquired compared the early days of their marriage when Bettie needed a bed and food. (Bettie's name is spelled several ways in the court documents, including Betsey and Betsy.)

> Betsey G. Andrews Plaintiff vs. George W. Andrews Defendant
> Complaint filed April 27, 1892
> *That plaintiff and defendant were united in marriage at Redwood City in the county of San Mateo State of California on the 24th day of September 1862 and ever since have been and now are husband and wife.*
> *That plaintiff at the County of Washoe in said State of Nevada and upon his ranch four miles south and west from Reno on the 24th day of April 1891 or there about did commit adultery with one Julia (so named) an Indian... in a house or structure thereon called "goat house."*
> *That defendant on or about 15th day of April 1888 at his said Ranch did commit adultery with the said Julia (so named) an Indian... in a building thereon called "Blacksmith Shop."*
> *That the defendant between the 15th day of April 1888 and the 24th day of April 1891 did at the said Ranch commit adultery with this said Julia (so named) an Indian... on diverse days and times to the plaintiff unknown at his camp at said Ranch when being in a tent thereon separate and apart from his family.*
> *Plaintiff alleges that each and all of said acts of adultery were committed without the consent, commission, procurement, or previous knowledge of plaintiff and that she has not lived or cohabited with defendant since....*
> *That since said marriage the defendant has treated her in a cruel and inhuman manner and in particular during the greater part of the time in the years 1888, 1889, 1890, 1891 and in 1892 to the time of commencing this action the defendant*

has used against plaintiff the most vile and profane language and epithets much of which language used by defendant upon and against the plaintiff is too obscene and vile to appear in her complaint or to have a place in the files or upon the records of a court. Some of the language used daily by the defendant against the plaintiff is as follows. "Aint you a d---ed curse of hell. G-d dam you" "You damed old bitch of hell – aint you a bitch of hell G-d dam you" "You damed old Irish bitch of hell. Aint that the way to talk to a bitch G-d dam you".... Following is language used by defendant to said plaintiff in the presence of their children "The Squaw is a d---ed sight better woman than you are G-d dam you. The Squaw is as good as you are You d---ed old bitch of hell."

Plaintiff shows that the continued abuse of the defendant has greatly injured her health. That mental anguish from continued neglect and abuse by him is destroying her bodily vigor and is speedily impairing her for the duties and responsibilities of life – that no other result will or can come of her but death and a premature Grave if her present relation to the defendant and present surroundings are continued.

Plaintiff for a further cause of action shows that the defendant George W. Andrews... since their said marriage has become and is now a drunkard.–

That he has become since their said marriage subject to habitual gross drunkenness contracted since their said marriage, incapacitates him from contributing his share to the support of the family. That he is disqualified the great portion of the time by the use of intoxicating liquors for attending to business, and is the most of the time unfit for the duties of life. That said habitual gross drunkenness is now upon him and has been upon him for more than three years last past.

Plaintiff shows that defendant is possessed of the following household and described property, real and personal, that all of said property has been acquired by the community and is common or community property. Next following is a list and statement of the personal property, including its values. Seven kitchen chairs 50 cents each $3.50, one set dishes $5.00, two cupboards $1.00 each $2.00, One Kitchen range $35.00, three parlor stoves $3.00 each $9.00, one kitchen stove $5.00, kettles and pots belonging to range $1.50, two pine bedsteads $5.00 each $10.00, one black walnut bedstead $8.00, one wardrobe black walnut $15.00, one parlor set $25.00, two chairs $2.00 each $4.00, one large easy chair $3.00, and lounge $5.00, three pictures in frames $12.00, three carpets $3.00 each $9.00, one piece matting $4.00, three rocking chairs $1.00 each $3.00, bedding and bed clothing $30.00, one buckboard $50.00, one cart $20.00, one cart $10.00, one parlor stand $1.00, one blacksmith outfit consisting of anvil, bellows, tongs, chissells and hammers $35.00, one kitchen treasure table $4.25, Six pitchforks, $4.50, two potatoe forks and two shovels 50 cts each $2.00, three grub hoes .75 cts each and two picks .75 cts each $3.75, one wash tub 50 cts and wash board 25 cts $.75, one homemade lounge $1.50, two home-made tables $1.00 each $2.00, one stutjars $1.50, three carpenters plains 75 cts each 2.25, three carpenters saws $1.00 each $3.00, three lamps 50 cts each $1.50, one stack of wheat $30.00, two road scrapers 5.00 each $10.00, twenty tons hay in barn $5.00 per ton $100.00, two flowerboxes, one $5.00 another $3.00 $8.00, dairy utensils, six pails 40 cts each $2.40, five dozen milk pans $12.40, Four milk cans and two cream jars $1.00, one churn $6.00. Sixteen head mulch cows $25.00 each $400.00, sixteen head of stock cattle 16.00 each $256.00, Seventeen head calves $4.50 each $76.50, Four head of work horses 80.00 *each $320.00, Seven head of mules 40.00 each $280.00, Ten head colts 20.00 each $200.00. One wagon $75.00, one wagon $40.00, one mowing machine $60.00, one mowing machine $15.00, one single cart harness $2.50, three sets of double team harness $35.00, Six shoats of young swine $30.00, one fat hog $15.00, four dozen chickens $4.50 per dozen $18.00. Eleven ducks 50 cts each $5.50, twenty tons of potatoes 8.00 per ton $160.00. Three cords of wood 3.00 each $9.00, three home-made rugs 1.00 each $3.00, three other rugs $10.00, Book case $5.00, one hay derrick and jack $25.00.*

The defendant is possessed of the following ... real property. [gives all the details of the land owned—very difficult to read]

Plaintiff shows there are two children surviving, the fruit of said marriage, a son and daughter, both of whom are of age, but have their home under the parental roof. B.H. Andrews the said son is now twenty-eight years of age, whose time and labour has been expended in the acquirement of much of the property above mentioned. Crissie Andrews the daughter of above mentioned is of the age of twenty four years who has given her time and labour to the acquirement of much of said property. B.H. Andrews claims he is a creditor of his father for work and labour performed for four years, ten months and fifteen days last past, which work and labour he claims is of the reasonable value of thirty five dollars per month. Crissie H. Andrews makes no claim for work and services performed. There are also other debts unknown in amounts unpaid.

Plaintiff because of the facts and causes of action above set forth prays the court that the marriage relation now existing between plaintiff and defendant be dissolved and set aside and that plaintiff be restored to the rights of an unmarried person. She also prays that she be decreed of the community property one half these of and which other greater portion thereof as equity and good conscience will allow and that she have her costs in the actions, expenses, and such other relief as the case will admit of.

April 26, 1892
Wm. Webster
City of Reno

Conclusions of Law
That the court concludes from the proofs and facts
That the defendant is guilty of extreme cruelty toward and against the plaintiff and that such cruelty has been continuous for the last four years.
And it is further ordered that the marriage relation now upon the plaintiff and defendant be and is dissolved and set aside and a decree to that said is directed and ordered.

Suzie, the Native American Indian who helped Bettie after Bettie's divorce from George.

It is also ordered and decreed that the community property of the said plaintiff and defendant there is decreed to the plaintiff the whole thereof both real and personal, subject nevertheless to such reservations and charges as are hereinafter stated and decreed. [following was a repetition of the list of property]

The real property of the community is described as follows, some of which real property is under contract from the state of Nevada and other portions of it is under contract with the Central Pacific Railroad Company. [again, the property was listed]

Also there is appertaining to the above described lands community property 150 inches of water flowing and to flow in Last Chance water ditch and 25 inches of water flowing and to flow in Southside irrigation canal and other waters used for irrigation and domestic purposes upon said lands.

That there is reserved to the defendant of the colts above mentioned two head which colts reserved may be by him selected from all the colts on the above mentioned premises and that have been heretofore owned by the community and the defendant. Upon such selection…other personal property above mentioned and all other personal property heretofore community property shall become and is the separate property of the plaintiff. The defendant shall have and receive from the plaintiff within thirty days from the date of this decree two thousand dollars in lawful money of the United States enforced.... It is also ordered and decreed that plaintiff according to the stipulation and fill in the action shall make a good and sufficient deed to Crissie Andrews daughter of the plaintiff and defendant forty acres of land known as the Mayberry forty acres together with the water used for irrigation on said lands being about twenty five inches of water as it flows.

In witness whereof the parties hereto and to said action have signed this agreement May 17, 1892

Suzie's house near the Truckee River on the Caughlin Ranch

A summons to appear in court was served to George W. Andrews on April 27, 1892 by Washoe County Sheriff William H. Caughlin. George's attorney responded "that the complaint does not state facts sufficient to constitute a cause of action against the defendant." The judge overruled the attorney, and George was required to answer the charges, which he did not do. A default was entered on May 9, 1892. In the end, George received $2,000 and two colts, Bettie kept the ranch, and Crissie inherited 40 acres on Mayberry.

Those were sad days for the Andrews, a family that was built on the seemingly solid foundation of love between Bettie and George. All the early dreams of their marriage were shattered. Crissie felt a tremendous sadness at the loss of her father, especially because she was her daddy's favorite. She always told me that when he was late coming home from the saloon, Crissie would fetch him in the "sulky," and drive the horse and buggy home with both of them singing at the top of their lungs. To Crissie, these were happy memories, and she always treasured the drawings he made as a young man that were displayed in their home. The social stigma that came with divorce was doubled for the Andrews family—having touched both Crissie and Bettie. However, the challenges of operating the ranch left little time for emotions. Benjamin was called home from college and became head of the family. He was to run the ranch and take care of his mother and sister, even though his business decisions didn't seem to measure up to his mother's expectations.

Bettie, Ben, and Crissie all pitched in, and for a time, it seemed they would manage to run the ranch without George. However, fate struck one final blow—one from which Bettie never recovered. The stark newspaper obituary told of the accident and Benjamin's tragic early death.

BROTHER BEN'S DEATH

Nevada State Journal
April 15, 1894
DIED ANDREWS – In Reno, Nevada, April 14, 1894, Benjamin H. Andrews, a native of California, aged 31 years.

A FATAL ACCIDENT
   Ben Andrews Died Yesterday From the Effects of a Kick by a Horse
   Benjamin H. Andrews died yesterday afternoon about 5 o'clock at the Andrews Ranch southwest of town from the effects of a kick in the abdomen by a horse received the day before.
   Dr. Hogan was summoned and did all he could to allay his sufferings but it was evident from the first that he had been fatally hurt. Yesterday morning Ben was told that he could not recover. He bore the news cheerfully and during the remainder of the day showed no fear of the great change in which he would solve the mystery of eternity.
   About 5 o'clock he began sinking and was unconscious for about ten minutes before he died.
   Deceased was born at Woodside, San Mateo county, California, in August, 1863, and removed with his parents from there to this State in 1865, where he has since lived. He went to school here in Reno, and also was a student for two terms in Napa College, where he took the commercial course.

Suzie and Bettie did laundry for others to earn extra money after Bettie's divorce from George

Suzie's house near the Truckee River on the Caughlin Ranch

He joined the Masons when he was 21, and has since been a member of that order.

Ben was well known in Reno and leaves a large number of friends to mourn his death.

The funeral will take place Monday under Masonic auspices.

FUNERAL OF B.H. ANDREWS

The funeral of Benjamin H. Andrews, whose sudden death from a kick by a horse on his mother's ranch cast a gloom over the community, took place from the Baptist church yesterday. The religious services were conducted by Rev. W.B. Pope and were very impressive. The singing, under the leadership of Mrs. B.F. Layton of the Episcopal choir, was sweet and solemn. The casket was covered with the choicest of flowers of the season. The funeral was largely attended. The procession was headed by Reno Lodge, No. 13 F. & A.M., of which deceased was a member, and the services at the grave were in accordance with the ritual of the Fraternity.

The deceased was a popular and highly esteemed young man, and sincere regret is expressed for his untimely death in the prime of health and vigorous manhood, and the sympathies of the community are extended to his bereaved relatives.

Benjamin Andrews, Crissie's only brother

The tragedies of the years from 1886 to 1894 tested Crissie severely. The man she first married was lost to a life of crime, and she lost their child. Then she lost her father to alcoholism, and her family was torn apart by her parents' divorce. Finally, her older brother was ripped away from her by this senseless accident, just when Crissie and her mother needed him most.

When I was a child, Crissie always told me that her mother died of a broken heart. Once all the pieces of this family puzzle fell into place, I could see why; her mother never recovered from the dual loss of husband and son.

With her father and brother gone and her mother devastated, Crissie, too, was left totally alone. She faced difficult choices. The ranch still demanded a steady hand, if Crissie and her mother were to survive. Although she had her college degree in business, the thought of running the ranch alone was overwhelming. Yet, Crissie's determination was solid as steel. The one constant in her life—the ranch—would remain in the family, no matter what the price. It was forever part of her strength.

CHAPTER SIX
Crissie's Marriage and Family

CRISSIE'S FAMILY was in shambles. After her parents divorced, Crissie's father George remarried and moved to Oregon. Her only brother was dead at 31, and she described her mother Bettie as a "basket case." Suddenly, Crissie was in charge of supporting her mother and herself and operating a ranch. Like many women of her era in similar circumstances, her choices were limited: labor to operate the ranch, sell the ranch and survive on the income, or marry a man who could help her save the ranch. Remembering her father's advice, "You keep the land and the land will keep you," Crissie opted to marry.

A WEDDING
Two of Reno's Best Known People Form a Life Partnership[1]

A quiet wedding took place at Andrews' ranch yesterday afternoon at 5 o'clock. The contracting parties were our Sheriff, W. H. Caughlin, and Miss Crissie Andrews, both of whom are well known in Reno and vicinity. Jack Caughlin, the genial Deputy Sheriff, acted as best man, and Mrs. Tucker of Verdi bridesmaid.[2] The ceremony was performed in an impressive manner by the Reverends Mr. and Mrs. Maynard.[3] The guests were limited to the families of the principals, and after the ceremony all sat down to a sumptuous wedding supper, the main feature of which was a wedding cake made by an aunt of the bride and sent from Delaware. The Journal extends congratulations and wishes Mr. and Mrs. Caughlin unlimited happiness and prosperity.

WILLIAM CAUGHLIN

No doubt Crissie knew Sheriff William Henry Caughlin, for Reno was a small town, and Washoe County records show he served the legal summons for divorce to George on April 28, 1892. Few of William Caughlin's letters were among those in Crissie's collection, but I found his biographical information in Nevada history books. Of Irish descent and born in Australia, he came to America with his family while still a child. He arrived in Nevada in the 1860s—about the same time as Crissie's parents.

William Caughlin's mother, Honora Caughlin

William Caughlin's father, William H. Caughlin, Sr.

He was born in Australia December 18, 1847, son of John H. and Honora (Higgins) Caughlin. His parents were natives of Ireland. In 1850 the family crossed the Pacific [from Australia] to San Francisco. John H. Caughlin died in 1852, and his widow survived him until 1902. William H. Caughlin had some schooling at San Francisco, learned the blacksmith's trade, and as a youth projected himself into the hardy activities that attracted the energies of strong men in the far West. He came to Nevada in 1864. His first location was at Crystal Peak.... Mr. Caughlin worked as a blacksmith and also participated in the other activities of various mining camps, both in Western Nevada, and in the Austin district and around White Pine. For some time he was located at Virginia City. But most of his years were spent in Washoe County.... In 1896 Mr. Caughlin gave up his shop in the city and moved to his ranch a few miles west of Reno.[4] There he engaged in general farming and raising of livestock.

... In 1895 Mr. Caughlin married Crissie H. Andrews.... one of the cultured and highly intelligent women of the state.[5]

Another profile of William included more information about his first marriage, his work as sheriff, and his social standing in the community.

A life-long Republican, Mr. Caughlin was elected sheriff of Washoe county for three successive terms upon the ticket of his party, and thus filled the office for six consecutive years [1891 to 1897]. Prompt and fearless in the discharge of his duties, he became a terror to all evil-doers and those who do not hold themselves amenable to law, and he succeeded in clearing the county of many desperate characters, arresting a number of men whose criminal records were very black. Property and life became more secure during his administration of the office, and he was accounted the most energetic, capable and reliable sheriff the county ever had.

In 1872 Mr. Caughlin was united in marriage to Miss Cornelia J. Sloan, a native of Indiana, and to them three children have been born: Arthur, who is now living in Reno; and Albert G. and Edward, both at home. The wife and mother died in 1883.[6] She was a most estimable lady, devoted to her family, faithful in friendship, and kindly in spirit. Mr. Caughlin remained single until 1895, when he was again married, his second union being with Miss Crissie

William Caughlin, born in Australia
Dec. 18, 1846

William Caughlin and Crissie Andrews courting, March 5, 1892

Crissie with her horse El Rose in front of William's Mill Street
House, c. 1895 or 1910

William Caughlin

H. Andrews, a most worthy and honored pioneer settler of the state.... Mr. and Mrs. Caughlin are well known in Reno and throughout the surrounding district, and their many excellent traits of character and sterling worth have gained them friendship and favor. An active business career dominated by honorable purpose and upright dealing, has brought to Mr. Caughlin a fair measure of success, and he now has large and valuable agricultural interests, which also demonstrate the richness of Nevada's soil for farming purposes.[7]

SOCIETY'S ACCEPTANCE

Crissie confided to me that she did not want to marry or have children after her first tragic experience. The only reason she married William Caughlin was to save the ranch. Less than a year after Ben's death, Crissie and William were married on February 12, 1895. In fact, Sheriff Caughlin was 19 years older than Crissie—nearly 50 and closer in age to her parents – a widower with three children, and a Catholic. Crissie was a divorcee from a Protestant background, so they had neither age nor religion in common. The shared interest that brought them together was the Andrews Ranch.

Crissie's second marriage was anything but a whirlwind romance. In fact, she said their courtship began with a wager. According to Crissie, Sheriff Caughlin and a friend were drinking in a bar, and both being widowers, they decided it was time for them to remarry. They discussed the list of eligible women, and William picked Crissie Andrews, hoping his children would inherit the Andrews Ranch. Caughlin's friend bet against the match, saying Caughlin would never convince Crissie to wed. Crissie often told me the story of their courtship, saying Caughlin was so ashamed of her divorce, that when he took her for a ride in his horse-drawn buggy, he cut through Reno's back streets and alleys. Ultimately, Caughlin won the bet and married Crissie, but he never owned the ranch.

In time, Crissie overcame the scandal of her first marriage and divorce, but she faced social ostracism from William's Catholic family and was never received by them. While sorting through one box of ranch records, I found evidence of the rejections Crissie faced. Mary P. Sloan, Cornelia's sister, evidently lived with William and cared for his house and children after her sister died. Perhaps she had hoped to take Cornelia's place as Caughlin's second wife. Her journal, written after she left the Caughlin home, seethed with her resentment of Crissie.

Laura Tucker, Crissie's friend, bridesmaid and photographer

William H. Caughlin

John Caughlin, oldest son of William and Cornelia Caughlin, Crissie's stepson.

Art Caughlin, son of William and Cornelia Caughlin, Crissie's stepson.

John Caughlin, 1896

Al Caughlin, son of William and Cornelia Caughlin, Crissie's stepson.

Mary Sloan and cousin, William's sister-in-law from his first marriage

September 9, 1895
Still sick. I thought I would never pull through last night. I really cannot say I care. I think I have suffered enough. I only hate to leave Eddie [Edward, William and Cornelia's youngest son and Mary's nephew]. How I wish I was rich and could have him with me. Poor children, how I pity them. But Bill is
happy and that is enough. Strange, my being away from the house makes him so happy and his home so pleasant. I could have left long ago.

How many times I have thought of the last time I was with Bill when he and Chris were home. Artie [Arthur, William and Cornelia's oldest son] called me in, and Chris drove up as I was coming away. As I passed out of the gate, not *one* ever said, "Come back. Good bye." In fact, nothing. I stood there quite a while, looking at Bill and Chris and thought it would be a *cold* day when I darkened their doors again or ever gave them a chance to smite me. And the very last time I was at the house was when I got my chairs, and Chris left word for me that, if I had any more old traps, to come and get them and never darken the doors again…. Bill even censures me, but that is as I expected—said I took all of poor little Neal's [Cornelia's] teddies, when I left them all.

I sent for Bill and Chris two days afterwards. Bill came, but I was too sick to talk. Dr. Hogan had just injected morphine for neuralgia of the heart. Poor doctor thought I would not pull through.

I don't want Bill or Chris to touch me when I am dead. If they can't come near me when I'm living, I don't need them when I am dead. If I don't leave money enough behind me to bury me, let the county bury me—not Bill Caughlin. I don't want any of his money when I am dead….

October 31
Doctor gave me some more medicine. Eddie, dear, came to see me. He gave me a bird that is a drawing. Tonight they are playing pranks. [Halloween] Today Artie and Rose have gone to the Forrester Ball.

April 27
Eddie Caughlin called in the evening and brought five little fish. Bless his little heart, he had no shoes on his feet, no vest on or overcoat. That is a stepmother, for when a man as old as Bill Caughlin forgets his children, it is about time he would go off and drown his old fool self, is my opinion. When love blinds me with such a looking husband as his wife, I hope God will strike me dead. [8]

In spite of the bitterness aimed at her, Crissie said she experienced many happy times during her marriage. At first, the Caughlin's lived in William's house on Mill Street near Virginia Street with two of his three sons, Albert and Edward. By summer, Crissie was pregnant with their first child, as Aunt Harriet confirmed in a letter.

Searsville, California
July 9, 1895

Dear Crissie,
 .... If it is a girl, call it after its great auntie. If it is a boy, call it anything you like. I don't care much for boy babies, I suppose. Well, I'll think it fine, no matter what gender it is....
 I see by your letter you are having a good time. Am glad you are. Hope your married life will be a happy one all through. Take good care of your mother. After the harvest is in, send her down. How I wish she would come. It would do her good and us too.
 Give my pious regards to your hubbie and take lots for yourself.
As ever your,
Auntie H.E. Hughes

CRISSIE'S PARENTS DIE

However, these early years of marriage were also punctuated with great sadness as the generation before hers passed away, one by one.

First, Crissie's mother died in 1896. Bettie lived just long enough to see her first grandchild, Bill Jr. Crissie always said, "My mother died of a broken heart," her health completely broken by years of hard work, the deaths of three of her four children, and the divorce from George.

> DEATH OF AN ESTIMABLE LADY
> Mrs. B. Andrews, one of Washoe county's early settlers and the mother of Mrs. W.H. Caughlin, passed away last night. She has been in poor health for some time, but her death was not looked for so soon. She had many friends in Reno and the valley who will be pained at the news of her death. Notice of the funeral will appear in the next issue.[9]

George lived fourteen years longer than Bettie, although it is doubtful Crissie ever saw her father again. Four months after Crissie's wedding, on June 1, 1985, her father married Mrs. L. [Lucinda] D. Moore and moved to Corvallis, Oregon.[10] When he died, the Reno newspaper ran a brief obituary.

Obituary, Died January 25, 1910
LIVED NEARLY 50 YEARS IN NEVADA
G.W. Andrews Western Pioneer Passes Away
in Corvallis, Oregon

Black paper cut-out of WIlliam Caughlin - a good likeness

Ruth Reed shot George Geiger, Southern Pacific trainmaster, west of Sparks at Caughlin Haystacks. Reno, July 25, 1915. Taken from Sheriff William Caughlin's photo album.

From W. H. Caughlin's

George Andrews pistol

Jack Davis, wanted in Idaho for murder, 1896. Taken from Sheriff William Caughlin's photo album.

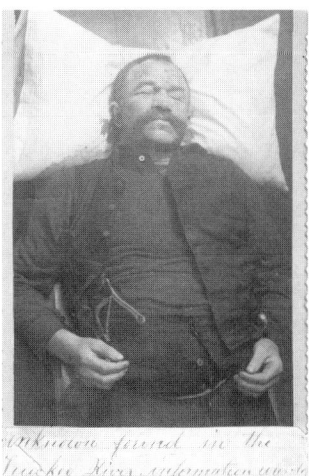
John Sontag, train robber, age 33 years, height 5' 11", dark hair and mustache, weight 165, lame in right ankle. Taken from Sheriff William Caughlin's photo album.

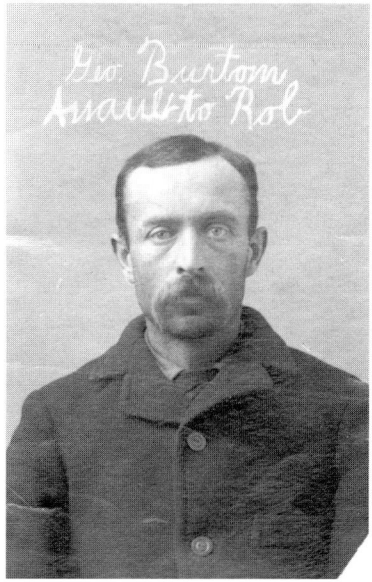
Unknown, found in the Truckee River, information wanted. Taken from Sheriff William Caughlin's photo album.

Wells Fargo box; the Wells Fargo stage drove past the Caughlin Ranch on the old Verdi Road.

George Burton, assault to rob. Taken from Sheriff William Caughlin's photo album.

Word was received in Reno yesterday by Mrs. Crissie Caughlin, of Andrews ranch, near this city, of the death of her father, George W. Andrews, one of the pioneer residents of Washoe county. Mr. Andrews died at Corvallis, Ore. Wednesday, at the age of 67 years, after an eventful life spent for the most part in the west.

George W. Andrews was born in Antrim, N.H. in 1843[11], and came to California in 1856, remaining there until 1862, when he removed to Washoe City, Nev. He then moved to a ranch three miles southwest of Reno, which has been known ever since as the Andrews ranch. He is survived by a sister who lives in Chicago, another in Antrim, N.H. and Mrs. Caughlin, the only living daughter.

Mr. Andrews is remembered by most of the older residents of this county who will hear with regret the news of his passing.[12]

Crissie composed a more detailed biography of her father's life, probably with the help of family historian Aunt Martha, who reported the Andrews family history at the annual French family reunions.

LIFE OF GEORGE WASHINGTON ANDREWS
b. February 10, 1834, d. January 10, 1910
by Crissie Caughlin

George W. Andrews, a pioneer and settler of Washoe County, Nevada, was born in Antrim, New Hampshire in the year 1834. Son of Benjamin R. Andrew and Hannah Blanchard, daughter of Greene and Molly (Page) French.

His early education was in the local schools and going to a new academy in New London, N.H. where he graduated, and was a civil engineer like his father before him. He taught school in several towns. In 1856 [at the age of 22] he got the wanderlust & came to California, going down the coast to the Isthmus of Panama, coming up the coast to San Francisco, going down to Half Moon Bay to teach a school. He worked in woods in the mountains in summer for Wm. Hughes who had a sawmill. Later Hughes & Andrews went to Aurora, Nev. where a gold rush was in progress [Crissie was mistaken—there is no record that George went to Aurora.] They made this trip in June & returned in October before the storms set in.

When he met Hughes' sister (Betsey Hughes) from Maine, they were later married,[13] returning to Aurora in 1862 [Again, Crissie was mistaken, since the letters indicate that George went to Virginia City and Bettie stayed at Silver Mountain City.] They located in Washoe City 1863, helping to get wood for the Virginia City Mines. In the early 1870s, there was quite a boom in Real Estate in the Truckee Meadows. He helped move the courthouse from Washoe City to Reno. Finally he looked for a location for a ranch. He found the place where his daughter now lives. Everything was taken on both sides. There was no water for this place. With the aide of a surveyor A.J. Hatch, they found they could get water out of the Truckee River about 4 or 5 miles. They immediately began excavating using men, horses, & scrapers. They named this ditch "The Last Chance Ditch" -- the last chance to take water out of the Truckee River this side of the state line between Nevada and California.[14]

Crissie learned of her father's death from his second wife, who sent a telegram. An Oregon coroner described her father's last years and suggested that Crissie help pay a final debt.

The Western Union Telegraph Company,
from Corvallis, Oregon, Jan 26th, 1910.
Cris Coughlin, [sic]
Reno Nev.
Your father died last night funeral tomorrow answer if coming.
Mrs. Geo. Andrews

The Western Union Telegraph Company,
from Corvallis Oregon, Jan 27th
Chris Caughlin
Reno, Nevada
Am in charge of remains of Husband, will bury here.
Mrs. Geo. W. Andrews

[letterhead of J.H. Everett Undertaker and Embalmer, Corvallis, Oregon] February 22, 1910

Mrs. Crissie Caughlin

Reno, Nev.
Dear Madam: It was I that prepared and buried your father. Am familiar with their circumstances. Your father has been unable to do any work for some time. Hence the support was left to his wife. Will say she has done well. She has paid for burial lot $10. Teams and carriages (2) $600. Is paying the Dr., has paid me $500, and has arranged for a Mr. Campbell to pay $50.00. Mr. C. had bought a horse or two from your father but was to have his own time to pay for them. There were several who wanted Mrs. Andrews to apply to the county for burial expenses, but she would not. Said, "she would work her fingers off first." My expense was $60.00. This included casket, hearse and nice black broadcloth robe. He was buried nice. I did not charge her for taking care of the body, which would have been ordinarily $15.00. I saw Mrs. Andrews today. She is going to place a tombstone to your father just as soon as she can earn the money. She is certainly true to him. I thought I would write you giving the true situation. So if you desired to help defray the burial expenses, you could send me the $50 yet due Mrs. A. from horses. If you desired to help us further she could use the amount to erect stone. Pardon me for saying so, but if you are financially able I really believe you ought. For Mrs. A. certainly has done her best. Trusting that you will appreciate this information rela-

Mary Andrew Cochrane left and Martha Andrew Byers right

Crissie continued correspondence with her Aunt Martha Andrew Byers, d. 1917

tive to your father's death and burial, I beg to remain.

> Yours very Truly
> John Everett.

Crissie sent a Wells Fargo & Company Express check for $100 in gold coin and received a receipt. The money went to Mrs. L.D. Andrews, Corvallis Oregon, March 16, 1910. Aunt Martha concluded that her brother's death was not the same as losing a close, cherished family member.

Chicago, Illinois
February 1, 1910

Dear Crissie,

Your letter came yesterday apprising me of the death of your father. I suppose we may rely upon the information, and as he has been the same as a dead relative to us for so many years, it seems not quite like losing out of your own midst one who has shown that he loves and desires to be loved by his own. I know George had his peculiar notions and when he went away from Reno, he said good-bye in his heart to all he left behind. He held no malice, I know, and he had his reasons for going and staying away from old associations.

Like you, he was to me a dear relative. I am sorry we could not have had a few last words with him. I shall never forget the last words of my mother as he stood on the doorstep of our birthplace, "the old red house on the hill." With tears in his eyes, he held her hand for the last time and she said, "Be a Christian." What he understood to be a Christian, we do not know. Nor do we know if he ever confessed Christianity – unless it has been since he left Reno.

I did want to go to Nevada when he was living there, but there were objections, and I did not. Had I any faith in a change after death, I would pray for him now, but "as the tree falls, so it lieth."

Lovingly,
Aunt Martha

[no date on this letter to Crissie's daughter]
Antrim, New Hampshire

My dear Elizabeth;
.... Your grandfather, my brother, when a little boy, found a baby woodchuck in a trap and brought it home and said, "I got him, grand sir." He had lugged it half a mile and surprised everybody. He was such a little boy to go off alone. It was not the last time he went off alone. When he was 21, he left our home in New London, went across to Panama, and up to the Golden Gate where he caged Miss Hughes and was so pleased with everything that he never came home to his mother and father again.... Onward was his motto....

So now good-bye and
love to all,
Aunt Martha

North Sutton, New Hampshire
August 8, 1910
Dear Crissie,
Next week is the French reunion.... I wish you could be with me. The house is there and some beautiful maple trees that your father planted when a boy. The granite steps up the terrace in front are still there.

This is where the reunion was held in 1906. If I did not send you a picture of it, let me know. That was the house in which your father was born and the window behind the crowd was where your grandmother used to look for the stage that she thought would bring back the only boy, the stage that brought his letters from a distant shore – letters which later ceased to come. And the mother died without seeing her lost boy again....

He was educated there [New London] and also attended school at Andover, New Hampshire, where he learned pen drawing, etc. He finished at New London and soon after went to California. He sailed to Panama, crossed the isth-

Crissie, 38, wearing black onyx and pearl pin that has been given to my daughter Syrene

mus by rail, I think, to Aspinwall, and sailed up the coast to San Francisco. Perhaps you know his history from that time....
Aunt Martha

Soon after her father and mother died, most of their brothers and sisters were also gone. Aunt Martha died of Bright's disease, an inflammation of the kidneys. After her death, Aunt Martha's children discovered lots of letters from Crissie: both Crissie and Martha had saved each other's letters as mementos of their strong friendship across the many miles that separated them.

Mrs. M. J. Byers
Passed Away at Her Home on
Main Street

After an illness of brief duration, Mrs. Martha J. Byers passed away at her home in Antrim on Friday, July 6th. [1917]....

Mrs. Byers was the daughter of Benjamin R. and Hannah French Andrew, and was born in New London May 23, 1841, at the old homestead of her parents and grandparents....

Miss Andrews received her education at the New London Academy, being among the first graduates of the institution now known as Colby college. In her early twenties she left New England for the South and while living in the state of Kentucky met Rev. Joseph H. Byers... whom she afterwards married....

She was instrumental in effecting the organization known as the Woman's Missionary Alliance, which represents the movement of the affiliated churches of Antrim to assist missions, and held offices in the local Woman's Relief Corps and W.C.T.U....

While by nature and personal preference Mrs. Byers was quiet and retiring, she seemed to possess unusual initiative in matters of moment, always allying herself with a just cause regardless of its favor or acceptance by a majority.[15]

One month later, Martha's sister Mary died of cancer. Although Aunt Mary did not correspond as frequently as Aunt Martha, Mary's daughter said Crissie was most like Aunt Mary:

You have never known her, but our cousins tell us that you are like her. She has been brave and cheery under circumstances that would daunt many better able physically to bear it. She has been father and mother both to us children and never failed us love and sympathy. She has held us up to high ideals and clean living. I wish you might have known her.
Winifred

Geographically, Crissie's closest relative was Bettie's brother, Uncle William, who died on Oct. 31, 1908. There is no record of his wife Harriet's death.

The life of Bettie's sister, Aunt Esther, and the history of the Circle H Ranch near Bridgeport, California, were recorded by Esther's granddaughter Millie

Hunewill Hamblet in her book, *The Saga of The Circle H* in 1961. When she sent the book to one of Crissie's children, she wrote:

> We grew up hearing about our *Aunts*, as we were always taught to call them – Betsy, Jane, Syrene, Harriet, and Uncle William. Aunt Hannah we knew well, as she came down from Bodie every so often, and (her son) Johnny Hearne, also. They were very gay and full of fun and we always enjoyed having them come. Aunt Hannah ran the County Hospital in Bodie for many years while Mr. Hearne was mining and in and out of Bodie. He was credited with having done much to develop the cyaniding process.
>
> Lucile says that the first Mr. Hughes was a widower with four children – Syrene, Jane, Betsy and William, when he married Rhoda Briggs (my great-grandmother). They had two girls, Esther and Stella. I know there were half-sisters and Uncle Wm. was a half brother, so I think four is right.... Stella, that was Aunt Hannah's real name.
>
> Do you know about the old letters your mother had – they must still be in her room in Bill's house. The last time I had a real visit with her, she brought out this big box crammed full of old letters. They were *really old* – 1860 and even earlier, I think, some of them. Some are from the East, some from Aurora. Your mother selected some at random and we read them aloud. They were just priceless! We had the best time reading them and how we did laugh over some of the things. All of the family had a grand sense of humor. You girls could probably find out anything you wanted to know about the family through them.
>
> Much love -- Millie

In addition to the deaths on Crissie's side of the family, two of William's brothers also died during this time period—Jack in November 1897 and Jerry in September of 1915. Their obituaries defined the role each of the Caughlin men played in Nevada history.

JOHN CAUGHLIN, AFTER A LINGERING ILLNESS,
PASSES AWAY

> John Caughlin, well known in Washoe county as a former Deputy Sheriff under his brother, ex-Sheriff Caughlin, quietly passed away at his brother William's residence yesterday afternoon at 3 o'clock. Jack, as he was familiarly known, has been failing in health for some months, and finally went out to his brother William's ranch, where he has received the tenderest care. Kind hearted as a child and as tender as a woman, has been the record of Jack's life.... In the discharge of his duties, he was firm yet always kind, and always had a word of sympathy for the worst criminal or most trifling tramp, but would perform his duty at any cost.
>
> John Caughlin was born in Australia, coming to America with his parents at the age of a little over a year. Had he lived until next month he would have reached the age of 48 years.
>
> He leaves an aged mother and two sisters, residing at Oakland, Califor-

nia, and two brothers Wm. H. and Jerry Caughlin of Reno, also a son and daughter. His son was with him during his last illness.[16]

ANOTHER PIONEER CROSSES DIVIDE

Former Employee at Carson Mint Succumbs After Illness of Over a Year

Jerry Caughlin, for close to 50 years a resident of Nevada, and for a quarter of a century a resident of Reno, passed away yesterday after an illness of over a year's duration. During his early life the deceased was engaged as a stationery engineer at nearly all of the big mining camps in Nevada and recalled many of the pioneer events in the Austin, Bodie and White Pine mining districts.

Later in his life, Mr. Caughlin accepted a mechanical position in the United States mint at Carson City. He was aged 69 years, 3 months and 20 days and was a native of Australia. The deceased was a brother of W.H. Caughlin of this city, Mrs. Dr. Wixom and Mrs. Linnie Ryder of Oakland, and uncle of Arthur, Edward, Albert, William, Syrene and Elizabeth Caughlin of this city.

The funeral services will take place tomorrow afternoon at 2 o'clock from the mortuary chapel of Groesbeck and O'Brien. Interment will be made in the Mountain View cemetery.[17]

Jerry Caughlin was a member of the Reno Wheelman at a time when bicycling was a favorite sport of Renoites.

RENO WHEELMEN

Perhaps the most enthusiastic celebration ever held at Reno was on the night of July 5, 1900, when the Reno Wheelmen arrived at Reno that evening after winning the Coast championship in a fifty-mile relay bicycle race from Sacramento bicycle team of ten riders at Sacramento on July 4, 1900. Four carloads of Renoites left Reno for Sacramento on July 3 and fully five thousand people witnessed the race at Sacramento and saw the Reno team win the championship from the Sacramento team. It was a great race from start to finish. The Reno team won by a margin of about one mile. There were ten riders for each team and each rider rode five consecutive miles.

After the race bedlam broke loose and the Reno Wheelmen were given the freedom of Sacramento. The policemen told the boys the city was theirs but advised them not

Jack Caughlin, William's brother

to break any windows. That night the celebration was terrific and the fireworks were immense.

The boys left Sacramento for Reno on July 5, and were enthusiastically serenaded and cheered as they passed through Verdi and when they arrived at Reno that night the ovation and reception was tremendous.[18]

Jerry Caughlin, member Reno Wheelman

Jack and Jerry Caughlin

Crissie with horse El Rose. She loved horses

Crissie with horse and buggy, dog Skidoo near the Ferris ranch, c. 1910. Photo by her friend Laura Tucker

Crissie, 46, Christmas 1915

Crissie, 49, 1917

Betsy and Crissie Caughlin at the ranch, c. 1938

Crissie dressed up to go to town, standing in front of the Ranch House, c. 1940

Betsy and Crissie, Easter Sunday, 1941

Century Club House, Reno, where Crissie was a member. She was also a memeber of the Garden Club

Sadie D. Hurst, Crissie Caughlin, Nell Hymers and Bessie Eichelburg, ready for an automobile trip

Changing a tire

John Dixon with four lady friends bound for San Francisco. Sadie D. Hurst, Nell Nymers, Bessie Eichelburg and Crissie Caughlin

John Dixon repairing a tire on the way to San Francisco in an old Dodge near the Truckee River

Wingfield, just over the hill from Aurora

Post office at Bridgeport

Same trip with photos of Grandma Crissie's Buick. Crissie learned to drive by getting behind the wheel and driving--no lessons

Highway in Smith's Valley along the Walker River

Photo from trip to San Francisco

CHAPTER SEVEN
Crissie Caughlin's Children

After Crissie's tragic first marriage and divorce, and the loss of her child, she never again wanted to marry or have children. However, when her parents divorced and her beloved brother was killed, Crissie was left alone with her sad, frail mother. The ranch was hers to operate. This was when William Caughlin came courting. A widower twenty years her senior with three sons, he wanted the Andrews ranch for his boys. Although Crissie married William, the ranch always belonged to her, and she was very much in charge.

Crissie told me she did not want children, but William was Catholic and had other ideas. "Your husband comes through your door. Your children come through your heart," she always said.

WILLIAM H. "BILL" CAUGHLIN, NOVEMBER 25, 1895 TO 1983

Nine months after the Caughlin's wedding, a Thanksgiving baby was born to Crissie and William—a son named William "Bill" Hughes Caughlin.[1] He was a healthy, happy baby; full of good humor and fun. They were living at the Mill Street house in Reno when baby Bill was born. Crissie enjoyed all her children. She had great patience and enjoyed watching their childish antics, but was not one to pick them up and hold them. Because most of her aunts, uncles, and cousins lived in the East and the South, she arranged for many professional photos of all of the children at regular two-year intervals.

SYRENE PEARL CAUGHLIN, JULY 12, 1898 – MAY 19, 1986

The second child and first daughter, Syrene Pearl Caughlin, was born July 12, 1898.[2] The Caughlin's were still living at the Mill Street house. Unlike her brother, who had dark hair, a dark complexion, and blue eyes, Syrene inherited her father's coloring. She was born with translucent skin, so white its appearance was like a pearl; hence her middle name. Her eyes were dark gray like her mother's, and her white-blond hair was straight and wispy. Syrene was small but strong, never idle, and had a great love for horses. Riding gave

Three generations, Crissie Caughlin standing, Bettie Andrews holding William "Bill" Caughlin, May 1896.

her a way to escape and spend time alone, away from her little sister, Betsy. Syrene could never confide in her sister, because Betsy would tell all.

When Syrene was older, she had even more animals, including a favorite dog named Bob and 25 cats. Her father took most of the cats, put them in a sack, and drowned them in the river. Being a very sensitive girl, she resented her father for this cruel act.

Like all of Crissie's children, Syrene had beautiful penmanship—which Crissie had learned from her father George. As art editor, she did the drawings for her high school yearbook. Syrene was an avid reader. Grandma Crissie's wonderful wit and sense of humor were passed on to each of the children. As the years passed, the children stayed strongly connected to Crissie. Grandma Crissie was always there for them, and the ranch house door was always open for anyone who wanted to "come home."

ROWLAND A. CAUGHLIN, MARCH 6, 1900 – JANUARY 12, 1914

Crissie's third child was born at the ranch on March 6, 1900. Not quite two years apart, Syrene and Rowland became as close to each other as twins, and with the same light hair, eyes, and complexion, they easily could have been twins. Their sensitive, quiet dispositions also matched, and they spent hours dreaming and playing together or enjoying the many farm animals that they both dearly loved. They especially loved horses and spent many happy hours riding.

ELIZABETH "BETSY" NORENE CAUGHLIN, MAY 12, 1902 – JANUARY 1999

The last daughter was born at the ranch in springtime, just as the fruit trees reached full bloom in the Truckee Meadows. The doctor was called to the ranch in the morning. After many hours of waiting, the doctor told Crissie to jump off the porch a few times to get things started.

Betsy had dark hair with red highlights, eyes that were dark green and amber, and a ruddy complexion like her brother Bill. To her father, she was the favored child. She was allergic to all the farm animals, so she could not join her older siblings in their play. Instead, she liked to play in the house with her dolls and dishes.

As she grew up and went to school, she continued to be different. She did not learn easily. Today her learning problem would most likely be diagnosed as dyslexia, but back at the

Bill Caughlin, 18 months, getting a doughnut out of a crockery jar.

William Hughes Caughlin, b. Nov. 25, 1895, 6 months old.

Bill Caughlin and friend

McKinley School 1909, Bill Caughlin 5th from left, middle row, with hand in coat.

McKinley School 7th grade, 1913, Bill Caughlin top right.

Syrene Caughlin

Syrene Pearl Caughlin

Bill and Syrene at the ranch, 1899

Syrene, age 5, 4th from left

Betsy and Syrene in Grandma Bettie's dresses, which are now in the Marjorie Russell Textile and Research Center

Betsy, Syrene and Rowland on the big rock at the Ranch house, c. 1905

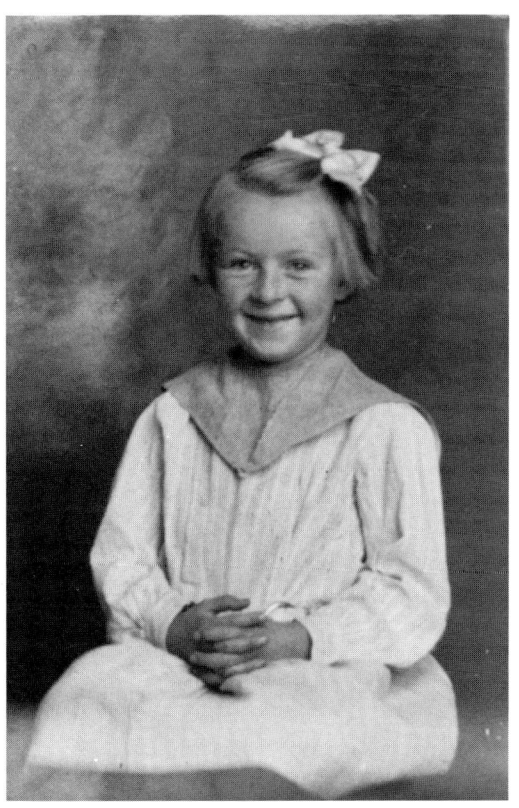

Rowland Andrews Caughlin, b. March 6, 1900

Rowland Caughlin, 1904

Crissie and son Rowland at the Ranch House, c. 1904

Rowland Caughlin, 5th from the left in middle row standing

Syrene and Rowland at the Truckee River, best friends

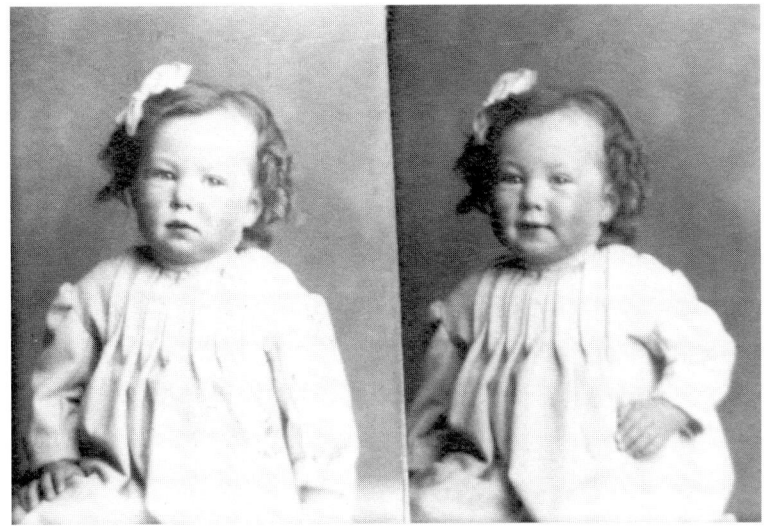

Betsy and kittens, c. 1910

Elizabeth "Betsy" Caughlin, c. 1904

Betsy Caughlin sitting on the rock with milking barns in background

Betsy and friend Peg play dress-up in dresses made of newspapers

Crissie, friends, Al Caughlin (dark shirt) and the four Caughlin children at a picnic, Donner Lake.

The Caughlin children, left to right, Rowland, Syrene, Betsy, William

Laughton School, c. 1907, Top row, left to right, Syrene Caughlin, Rowland Caughlin, Joe Rosasco, Earnest Capurro. Botton row, Frank Avancino, Gus Capurro, Bill Caughlin, Elizabeth Caughlin, teacher Mina Capurro. Little girl in front, Mary Gardella

Bill, Betsy, Rowland, Syrene, and a friend on the big rock petting dog Bob

turn of the century, she simply didn't finish anything she started—such as completing schoolwork.

Betsy had a natural talent for drawing and painting, a talent she shared with her sister Syrene. Syrene was invited to join the plein-air watercolor class with the well-known California artist and teacher, Lorenzo P. Latimer. He came to Reno every spring and fall to teach his watercolor methods to young ladies. Crissie would not let Syrene join without taking Betsy along, and Betsy painted all of her lifetime.

Betsy had many friends throughout her life. When she was older, she took piano and violin lessons and had a natural talent for music. She never wanted to have children, and instead she spent her energy mastering the culinary arts and earning a reputation as an outstanding cook.

DONNER LAKE VACATIONS

When Bill was about 8½ years old, Crissie took all of the children to Donner Lake for a vacation. William stayed behind to run the ranch and sent these letters to Crissie. In both he both expressed affection for the children, and one contained news of an accidental death in Reno.

At Home
July 5th, 1904

Dear Crissie,
Received both of your letters. Was glad to know that you got to the lake safe and that you all are having a good time. Every thing is as you left them—all OK at home. Pete is cook and I wash the dishes, sometimes, so be sure and let me know when you start for home that I may have a chance to wash all the dishes and sweep the floor by the time you get here.
… Kiss them all for dad. Let me know when you start for home. Do not hurry home on my account, but stay as long as you are enjoying yourselves.

Yours Sure, Bill

At Home
Aug. 7th, 1904

Dear Crissie
Yours of the 5th received this morning. I will say you are more than good for writing so often. It does me good to hear from you and the babies and to know you are having

William, Crissie and Betsy, picnic at Donner Lake

William and Crissie (seated) with a friend at Donner Lake

Betsy at the Truckee River, 14

a good time. The weather is very hot here. It is very cloudy but no rain. Mrs. Sharron, the old lady that cooked on the Sparks Ranch, will be buried tomorrow. She went to town Friday with Bob Eason and got too much beer and would not go back to the ranch with Bob. So he went home and left her in town. About 12 o'clock that night, she went to Homer's Stable and tried to get them to take her to the ranch…. could not get anyone to take her home, so she said she would walk and started off, but got on the wrong track and was found the next morning in the ditch that runs through Mrs. Judkin's back yard. She floated down the ditch and was caught on that water wheel. Mrs. Cornell, Mrs. Judkin's daughter, seeing the wheel in the ditch had stopped, went to see what was the matter and found the old lady fast in the wheel. She was dead when found and will be buried tomorrow. She has two sons and a daughter…. I had some visitors come to see me to day, but I left Jerry with them to entertain…. my company was still there when we got home…. They brought their own dinner with them and had a nice time on the bank of the river at the lower end of the ranch

Criss be sure and tear this up when you read it – if you can read it. If you can't, bring it home and I'll read it for you. Tell Syrene that her letter was fine and that she must write to me again.

Everything is all right here. The wheat will be ready to cut the last of this week. Take good care of the babies and kiss them for Dad. Tell them Dad said he would like to go up and see them, but I can't get away.

With love and a kiss to you all. Good night.
 Dad
 WHC

Fewer letters survived from this period in Crissie's life, no doubt because all of her closest aunts had passed away and because Crissie had her hands full with four small children under the age of 8.

ROWLAND'S DEATH

Some of the most tragic letters Crissie saved were those written from San Francisco in 1913. Her son Rowland had been very ill with what was most likely rheumatic fever. Crissie took him to see Dr. Asa Weston Collins, her cousin by marriage to Minnie Hughes, and another specialist in San Francisco. Crissie and Rowland stayed with the doctor (or Pa as most of the family called him) and Minnie during that time and wrote to William back at the ranch.

(undated)
3303 Sacramento St., S.F.

Dear Dad,

I am back in the city.... I had a long talk with Dr. about Row. He says he can't tell for a few days, but he thinks his lungs are in a bad way. He has given him medicine for his heart and that is doing fine. He still has that bad cough. We are trying to heal and stop that. He thinks I may have to take him farther south where it is warmer. This doesn't look encouraging, does it? I nearly had a nervous chill when he told me that. He looks much better, has gained three pounds this week. Don't write anything back. I don't want to worry him, and I'll take the best care of him. He is young and has a good constitution and with good care, will come out all right.

Will write you nearly every day.

With love to you all,
Criss

Nov. 8, 1913
San Francisco

Dear Dad,

Received your letter this a.m. Row is very much better the last three days. His cough is leaving him fast. His temperature is getting to normal. Last night is the first night he has not had night sweats. Dr. Mardis and Dr. Collins both say his heart is enlarged. He can't live in Reno. Well, we will talk about that when I get home. I will be there soon, about Thursday morning. I am very glad you have a good opportunity for renting. We will go down to Redwood and stay right there. Then the children will be in school and we won't have to pay rent.... I just feel fine to see him improve.

Everything will come out OK. Don't Worry.

Yours with love,
Criss

(on letterhead of Dr. Asa W. Collins)
3303 Sacramento St., San Francisco, California
Nov. 22, 1913

Dear Dad,

We arrived here safe Thursday morning about nine o'clock, and about ten mama started for Mayfield and said she would be back that night. But she changed her mind and said she would be back next Thursday night instead. I am feeling fine and have gained one pound.

From Rowland

Dec. 2, 1913

Dear Dad,

I received your letter. I was pleased to hear from you. I am feeling fine. My heart is not jumping half as hard as it was when I was home. I wrote to Al day before yesterday…

From your son,
Rowland Caughlin

Dec. 2, 1913

Dear Dad,

Row has written you a few lines, so I will put in a few words. I can't tell just how he is. One day I think he is fine and perhaps the next day he is all in. Today, I had to fight with him to get him out. We went up to the children's play ground and stayed all afternoon. I could hardly get him to go back home. He has an awful cough. Dr. is giving him medicine for his heart and cough medicine too…. Row scares me. He has a little fever every day. I did not bring my thermometer, so I don't know how high it runs. He has those bright red spots on his cheeks, and then again he looks so bad, it scares me. I know I don't realize how bad he was. Well, I am doing all I can for him. His appetite was pretty good today.

With love to all
Your Ma

Antrim, N.H. Mar. 12, 1914
Dear Crissie,

It is hard for me to say anything to comfort you, and yet I do want to. I have thought so much about you and wish my arms were long enough to draw you to myself, so you could feel my heart beats for you. I was so afraid you might lose another boy when I learned of his sickness and how risky he was to get out of bed to wait on himself….

Aunt Martha

The worried, but hopeful letters from Crissie stopped when Rowland died, January 12, 1914. When Aunt Martha said "you might lose another boy," she was referring to the death of Crissie's first baby—the only reference to Crissie's baby by George

Brown that I found among all of her letters. Aunt Martha knew what deep sorrow Crissie would feel, and Crissie's grief must have been prolonged by the fact that Rowland was not buried until spring when the ground thawed. Years later, upstairs in his room at the ranch house, I found a box of marbles and children's toys that belonged to Rowland. When I showed them to her, Grandma Crissie cried. "You can lose a husband or parents, but you never recover from losing a child," she told me.

RENO BOY DIES AT SACRAMENTO
    Rowland Coughlin (sic) Succumbs
    to Attack, Heart Failure
    After Short Illness
    Rowland A. Coughlin, son of Mr. and Mrs. William Coughlin, residing at the family ranch near Laughtons, died Monday evening at Sacramento after an illness of several weeks. The youth, who was aged about 14 years, was taken ill with heart trouble and several days ago was removed to Sacramento in the hope that the climate change would prove beneficial.
    The boy was a native of Nevada and is survived by his parents, four brothers and two sisters. The remains will arrive from Sacramento aboard train No. 6 this morning and will be accompanied by the parents. The funeral services will be announced later. William Caughlin, the father, was formerly sheriff of Washoe county and is one of the better known pioneer residents of this state.[4]

    CAUGHLIN—In Sacramento, January 12, 1914. Rowland A., dearly beloved son of Mr. and Mrs. William Caughlin and brother of William Jr., Elizabeth, Syrene, Albert, Edward and Arthur Caughlin, aged 13 years, 9 months, 6 days, a native of Nevada.
    Funeral services to be held from the chapel of Groesbeck & O'Brien, Friday afternoon at 2 o'clock, Rev. Mr. Adams officiating. Interment Masonic cemetery.[5]

BILL, THE LATER YEARS

In some ways, Crissie lost all three of her sons—the baby that died at birth; Rowland, who died at 13; and Bill, whose adult life can only be described as tortured. The happy boy was not a good student in school. His father always put him down and favored his sons from his first marriage. The verbal abuse turned Bill into an insecure child. As a young man of 21, he joined the U.S. Navy to fight in World War I. Bill asked in one letter, "Is Dad on the war path and does he still pay all the bills?"

Rowland, left, on Billie, and Bob Carter on Old Kate

Left to right, Duey Plumb and Bill Caughlin, U.S.S. Huntington, World War I.

Young Bill shipped out to Europe on the U.S.S. Huntington and, although he was gone only two years, he and his crew saw plenty of action. By April of 1919, Crissie petitioned for Bill to be discharged, so that he could return home and help his 72-year-old father with the ranch. The petition said he planned to attend the Agricultural College of the University of Nevada; however, when Bill returned, it was apparent he suffered from severe "shell shock." Although he spent the rest of his life at the ranch, he was not capable of operating it.

He worked on the ranch, rode horses, mended fences, hunted and fished with his friends and neighbors, the Schiappacasse brothers, Mike and John. Bill volunteered his time and was very active at the Veterans Hospital. Once he dated a woman for a brief time, but she drank a great deal, and Bill didn't like feeling ill from the alcohol, so he never married or had children.

When I was small, I remember Uncle Bill as a very rude person, especially to family members and children. I think their childish noise must have rattled his fragile nerves. A tall man at 6 feet, he remained thin, and his arms and legs jerked involuntarily. His dark brown hair turned gray as he aged, but he kept his ruddy complexion and strikingly blue eyes. In his later years, he was a ward of the court and his sisters were his guardians.

Left to right, Syrene, Jack the dog, Crissie sitting, Betsy, with Art Caughlin driving and William Caughlin in passenger seat of car. On the way to Donner Lake

Wabuska, Nev. [Lyon County, near Yerington]
Dec. 3rd, 1918

Dear Crissie,

I have let the time slip by and haven't written to you from here. I hope you have all escaped the "flu," and that you are well as usual. Are the girls back in school again?

Aurora has closed down....

So far we have all kept well, but the "flu" as you have seen by the papers, has been raging terribly in Virginia [City]. Since I left, also in Smith Valley and in Yerington. I hope to hear from Millie again today; they were both well and Charles was taking the serum treatment when she wrote last; Stanley was down here the first of last week, and he said they expected to take that treatment at the ranch up at Wells; Dr. Brown has been so busy.... It seems terrible to think of all the deaths of friends....

What do you hear from Bill? Isn't it grand that the war is over? Or is it over? Must we have to lick the Kaiser again? I hope everything will be fixed up all right, but they should wipe the whole German nation off the face of the earth.... Did I tell you Harry was in the big drive the last of September and first of October, and didn't have a face mask or have his shoes off for nine days and nights?...

        Alice Hunewill

SYRENE, THE LATER YEARS

My mother ultimately gained a measure of independence from the ranch, because she suffered from allergies and spent part of each summer in San Francisco with Dr. Asa Weston Collins and Aunt Minerva Hughes Collins, Crissie's cousin. Dr. Collins was a brilliant surgeon and head surgeon at the French Hospital in San Francisco. The French Legion of Honor recognized him for performing surgery under a man's heart, while holding the heart in his hand.

Dr. Collins and Aunt Min were like a second set of parents to all of Crissie's children, especially Syrene and Betsy, who were sent to stay with them each year during the haying to escape hay fever season. The difference between cold, snowy winters at the ranch and the elegance of city living changed Syrene. This was the life to which she aspired—with its beauty, culture, and mild weather. Pa (as they called Dr. Collins) and Min were life-long mentors to all of Crissie's children and grandchildren.

When Syrene was ready to go to college, she started at the University of Nevada, but attended there only a short time. Her father, unlike her mother, did not think it was proper for girls to have a higher education, so she left home and went to live with Pa and Min. With Dr. Collin's encouragement, she went into nursing.

When Ed Seagrave from Alameda visited one of her hospital patients, who was his best friend, he met my mother Syrene and invited her to go out to dinner. They were married within three days. They had two children—a boy named Asa Weston and me, Shiela Marion Seagrave. We were both born in San Francisco and delivered by Dr. Collins at the St. Francis Hospital.

My parents had an exceptional marriage and a great admiration for each other. They were always happy and laughing. My father adored my mother. My brother and I were Crissie's only grandchildren, and she came to visit us often. My father and Crissie were also very close. She depended on him for sound advice. Everyone loved my father, even Uncle Bill Caughlin. Ed had a great charisma and never met a person he didn't like or who didn't like him.

After a 35-year career with the Paraffin Company in San Francisco, he retired and my parents moved to Reno. He started a new company in Reno, Nevada Building and Supply Company. In two years, he doubled his investment in that company.

Betsy and Syrene

Betsy Caughlin, 1936

Betsy Caughlin, 13,
Christmas 1915

Betsy Caughlin with horse, 1914

Betsy wearing Red Cross scarf

Betsy Caughlin, 2nd from right, with friend. Her first husband, Howard "Dinty" Moore on the left

Betsy and Roger Donnelly, 1937

Betsy at the Ranch House, 1998

My parent's love story had a sad ending for our family when my dad died of a stroke at the young age of 55. My brother Weston and I were adults. Weston was serving in the U.S. Air Force in Europe, and I was performing in the musical play, "Straw Hat," after spending two years in New York studying voice. Mother went to work selling real estate. Five years later, she married Tony Cataldo. They traveled and enjoyed life together for a while, but mother did not feel they were compatible and left him. She lived to the age of 89, but she was devastated by my father's death. She never completely recovered from losing him.

In later years, my mother remained active. She always loved her flower garden and playing bridge. (When my father was alive, they had started a bridge club with some of their close friends.) She also learned to play golf in the 1930s.

My mother was a soft-spoken woman of few words, and she had a dry, quick wit—always making funny little comments under her breath. She was always kind, and nothing bothered her. She could "go with the flow" and have fun.

BETSY, THE LATER YEARS

Betsy married at the age of 20 to Howard "Dinty" Moore. She told me she didn't love Howard, but her parents had made all the arrangements, and her mother had baked a cake. She and Dinty had many friends, and they liked to party and drink a lot. They were married 10 years, divorced, remarried, and divorced a second time. In 1935, she married Roger Donnelly. They had no children, so she always supported my singing career, adored my children, and treated them as if they were her own.

The Caughlin Ranch was very important to Betsy. She did not want to sell any part of it. The three children—Bill, Syrene, and Betsy were left the entire ranch in undivided thirds. Bill was a ward of the court and the two sisters were his guardians. A large amount of the ranch property had to be sold to pay the taxes when Crissie died.

CHAPTER EIGHT
Crissie's Ranch
The Andrews/Caughlin Ranch

WHEN NEVADA MINING hit hard times in the late 1800s and the railroads routed commerce away from Washoe Valley, Crissie's father George Andrews turned to ranching to support his family. He hoped, along with others, that raising livestock and hay would revive Nevada's economy.[1] While agriculture did not replace mining as Nevada's leading industry, it did improve the Andrews family fortunes.

George first acquired the land on the Old Verdi Road, located between what is now Plumb Lane and Mayberry Street, in 1874, according to one of Crissie's journals. She said George earned some of the land in exchange for designing the Steamboat and Last Chance water irrigation ditches. He also received free water rights for his land, an issue that was later disputed during Crissie's ownership and operation of the ranch.

In addition, George may have purchased at least part of the original ranch from the checkerboard of land owned by the railroad. Crissie's correspondence shows a debt to the Central Pacific Railroad Company that still existed after her father and mother divorced and George left the ranch. Crissie made the payments on interest and principle, paid off the debt, and continued to buy more land over the years.

The Andrews ranch was one of several that were owned by early Washoe County ranchers. The now-familiar last names included Plumb, Wheeler, Lake, Frey, Sparks, Newlands, Thompson, and others. Today, these pioneers' names are on subdivisions and streets throughout the Truckee Meadows.

George raised alfalfa to feed his animals, and it was his main cash crop. He raised horses for transportation and to work the ranch and he also raised cows, hogs, chickens, and sheep for food and for sale.

Crissie's mother gave the ranch to her. As expected, Bettie Andrews willed the ranch and all her property to her only surviving child.

BETTIE'S WILL
Ranch, Jan. 15, 1896

At my *death* I give and bequeath to my only living child, Crissie Andrews Caughlin, or her children all that I may die possessed of, Real Estate and Personal Property, Notes and Insurance Policies, Horses, Cattle Wag-

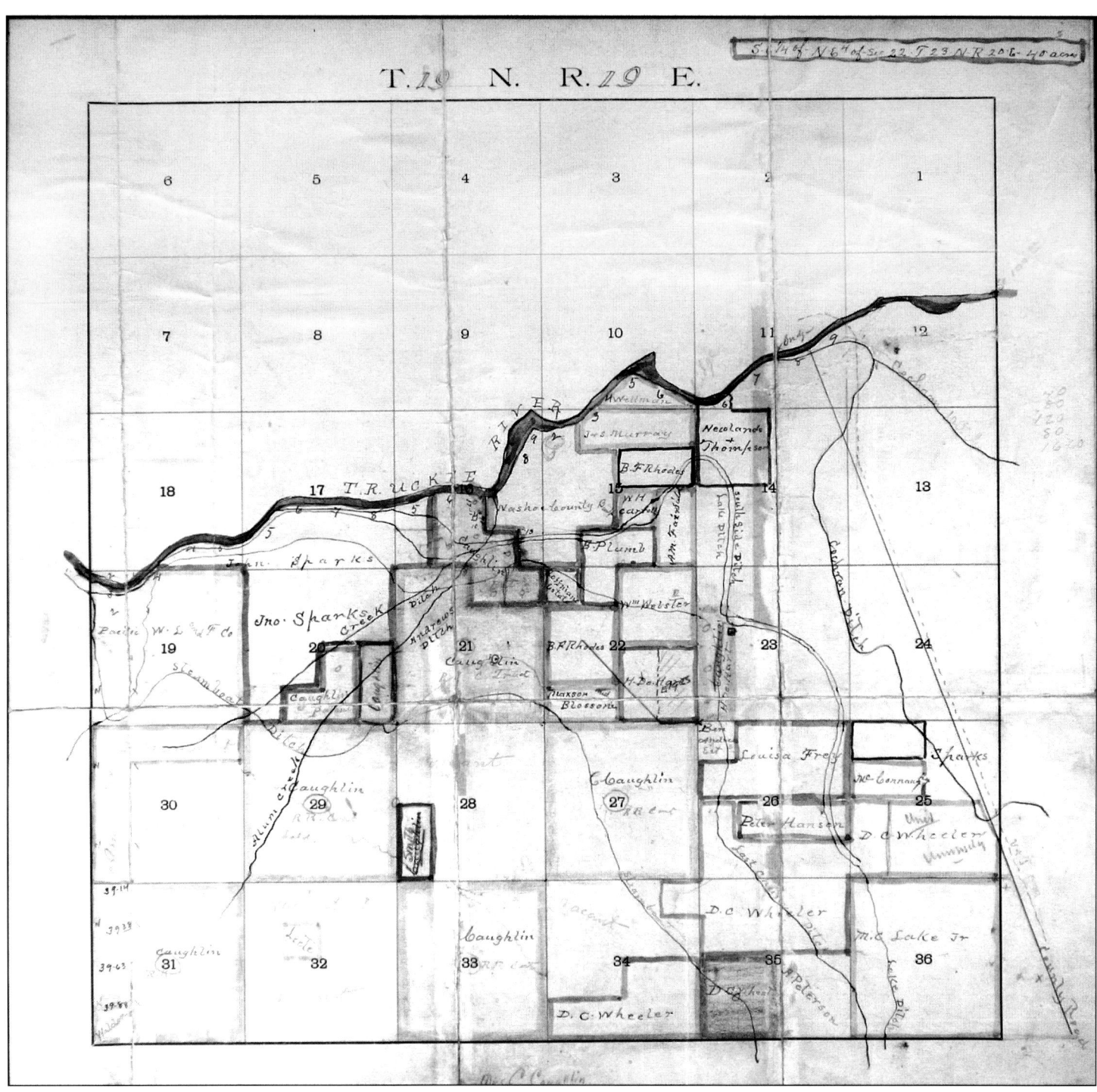

Map showing the Caughlin Ranch and other adjacent properties, ca. 1900

gons, Harnesses, (every thing) without Administration or Bonds; I have no one else to claim any thing of mine. See to Jane Hughes Powell and allow her to live in her Place as long as she lives or is capable of taking care of herself.

Betsy G. Hughes Andrews.
Ranch, Jan 15, 1896[2]

John Schiappacassi, nearest neighbor and good friend with young Bill Caughlin, c. 1929 at Caughlin Ranch

Tax records show the ranch had grown to 3,070 acres in 1897, and with $500 in improvements and $470 in personal property, the total value was $6,115.00. Taxes assessed to Mrs. Crissie Caughlin came to $123.61. In comparison, William's Mill Street house was worth $900. Bettie's sister Jane lived near the Truckee River in a home that was worth $900. Records show Jane borrowed $800 from Crissie against the value of the house.

The ranch was really more like a farm, since the only grazing cattle were on land that Crissie rented to others. The haying operation consumed the summer months, often taking six to eight weeks of time and extra hired hands. Photographs of haying were taken in the lower meadow, between the ranch house and the river. Aunt Esther Hunewill described the challenges of finding and keeping hired hands at haying time in one of her letters.

August 13th [year unknown]
Wellington, Nevada

Dear Crissie,

We finished haying two weeks ago today, and Stanley started to the other ranch with teams and men to do the haying there, but we do seem to have the worst luck of anyone I ever knew…. When we were a little more than half through haying, our men (the poorest crew we ever had – they just tried to see how little they could do) thought they would strike for higher wages. They were getting $1.75 per day. They told him they couldn't work any longer for that—they must have $2, so he told them he would have to stand it for the time being.

Stanley went down this valley and rustled up a new crew, and when they came in at night, he paid them [the original crew] off, and such a crest-fallen set of men you never saw. They went down the road with their blankets on a horse and donkey….

Two weeks ago tonight three of the boys that were working here went to town and from there to the Indian Camp. The Indians were drunk and fighting and drove them off.

John Schiappacassi

The gang and the 1923 Buick, John Scheppacassi, Tom Plum, Jim Mesconi, Mike Schiappacassi and Buck Pieretto

The big ranch house moved from Virginia City

Betsy and Syrene with ranch hand Joe Rondo between them, standing on a horse-drawn reaper

The next day, these three and some more of our men went with Stanley to the other ranch for haying. The next morn (Tuesday) the Indians living just above us (who had been away some days and just got home) came on the run for Lucile to go up, as

there was a dead Indian in the shed up there. Lucile and Millie went right up and the Indian was there. Lucile came home and phoned to the coroner, and the others and finally got a crowd together. It proved to be the Indian that was drunk and fighting when these boys were there. Someone swore out a warrant for these boys for murdering the Indian and—if Stanley hadn't worked day and night to clear them—they would have been bound over. They tried them for two days and found there wasn't a scrap of evidence against them, so were forced to turn them out, and they got back to haying after about a week's delay.

I thought you would come over this summer after you got a car and while the children could come with you. We have only two men on the ranch now, the gardener and the irrigator, but the crew will be back the last of the week. Then we will have to have a double crew, as the grain is all ready to cut.

Love to you all
from Esther

About two or three years after their marriage, the Caughlin family moved to the Andrews Ranch. Although it became known as the Caughlin Ranch, Crissie told me that ownership of the land remained in her name—somewhat unusual at the turn-of-the-century when women could not yet vote and had few legal rights. In fact, one of William's early biographers assumed that he owned the land.

> An active business career, dominated by honorable purpose and upright dealing, has brought to Mr. Caughlin a fair measure of success, and he now has large and valuable agricultural interests, which also demonstrate the richness of Nevada's soil for farming purposes.
>
> ... he came to his present location in 1896, having determined to put aside the duties of the smith and turn his attention to the tilling of the soil. He has a fine farm of two hundred acres pleasantly located a few miles west of Reno, and he also owns a side range of six hundred acres. He is now engaged in the raising of grain and stock, and upon his place are large and substantial barns for the shelter of his cattle. The hay, which he cuts annually, is fed to his stock, and the latter is sold at a good price upon the markets so that his labors bring a good return and make him one of the men of affluence in this locality. In 1900 he erected his fine residence, a modern home with splendid appointments and pleasing surroundings.[3]

William was responsible for the "fine residence"—the big, two-story house that still sits at the corner of Mayberry Street and McCarran Boulevard in Reno. Crissie's father George built the original ranch house by hand where Crissie and her brother Benjamin grew up, a small building that later became the bunkhouse. However, the original ranch house was too small, for the Caughlin's family had grown to seven people—two of William's three sons were still at home and were joined by the first two children born to William and Crissie—William Jr. and Syrene.

From the time I can remember, Crissie told the story of how the big house was moved from Virginia City to the ranch. Back then, it wasn't unusual for houses to be moved from one town to the next, because lumber was such a scarce and precious commodity. Smaller houses were often moved on a horse-drawn, flatbed wagon. However, Crissie said the ranch house was so big that it was taken apart in Virginia City, hauled to Reno, and reassembled on the present site.

The big ranch house faced Verdi Road, which passed near Crissie's front porch and ran parallel to what is now Mayberry Drive in Reno. It dissected the ranch into two parts known as the upper and lower ranch. Verdi Road was a main thoroughfare, often used by Wells Fargo stages, and the remains of the old roadbed can still be seen in the pasture just inside the fence

Mike Schiappacassi on horse at Caughlin Ranch barn. You can see South Verdi road, now Mayberry Street, and hay wagons in the background

Haystack on Caughlin Ranch with William and Betsy standing on the left

Haying operations at the lower Caughlin Ranch between South Verdi Road (Mayberry) and the Truckee River where River Run and Stonegate developments are now

on Mayberry Drive.

The house had two parlors—a front parlor for formal entertaining and a back parlor for more informal gatherings. The master bedroom was also at the front of the house, and in that room Crissie kept William Caughlin's 1856 Colt Navy "Peacemaker."

My memories of the ranch as a four-year-old child are still like a movie picture in my mind. The two-story ranch house had so many wonderful hidden treasures to discover. One was the music room with its large square piano and the very old sheet music that Grandma Crissie used to play. She sang, but mostly she whistled, a very deep and melodic sound, much like her speaking voice.

All the walk-in closets held a trunk. I think there were seven of them. Just off Crissie's bedroom was a dressing room where she kept her mother's large trunk made of wood and painted tin embossed in silver and gold leaf designs. Inside were dark red compartments covered with printed paper, like wallpaper, with pictures of ladies' faces and figures in many different styles of dress and lingerie. It held unusual wooden trays that could be removed. In the trunk I found a child's black and white shoes, about 4-inches long. The box they were in said, "Betsy's shoes. Along with the shoes I found four very small, white babies' christening dresses.

ADVENTURES AT THE RANCH

As a small child, I knew it was summer when we arrived at the ranch for our annual vacation. Grandma Crissie was there to greet us, holding the screen door open, eyes sparkling, and she was grinning from ear to ear. Her apron reflected the day's chores—chicken feathers from cleaning chickens and flour from making a pie or sour cream cookies.

I remember the wonderful meals my grandma made for us. Each year, the fruit trees produced plenty of apples, and the garden supplied potatoes, carrots and other vegetables that were canned or stored in the cellar. Crissie sold eggs, chickens, and homemade butter to the townspeople, just as her mother had. On Sunday, she would grab a big hen, wring its neck, chop its head and feet off, slit it open and feed all the guts to the many ranch cats. Then she would throw it into a pot of boiling water to loosen the feathers for plucking.

Her kitchen had a large, enameled wood stove, which Crissie kept hot most of the time with wood she chopped and stacked in the large bin next to it. The stove was also the only source for hot water. As children, we were sent to the nearby field to pick fresh sweet corn and shuck it. The corn was dropped into a pot of boiling water and, in what seemed like just 5 minutes, dinner was served featuring fresh corn on the cob. The table was always filled with many dishes in large bowls—always boiled potatoes that smelled of ground pepper. The fresh chicken might be stewed, fried, or roasted. Bon appetite!

Almost all of the food was grown on the ranch. Fruits and vegetables were exchanged with nearby neighbors. The Ferris Ranch had a large peach orchard, an indelible memory for me, because the peaches were made into ice cream on the Fourth of July. The Schiappacasse's ranch was the nearest, and the two families shared their bounty in summer and canned even more for the winter. Crissie prepared chickens and wild game—quail, doves, venison, and minced meat. Johnny and Mike always loved Crissie's pie crusts; she made them with bacon grease. The Schiappacasse's had an endless supply of sweet strawberries, and Grandma Crissie whipped cream with a fork to pour over the berries. Mrs. Schiappacasse also made mouth-watering spinach raviolis, but only for special occasions like Christmas and funerals.

In the early days, the pie safe was the only refrigeration at the ranch. It stood six feet high with screened sides. Fresh eggs were kept on top of dish towels in a bin of the cabinet. When I was a little girl, there was also a wooden ice box at the bottom of the steep stairs to the cellar. It held a 10-pound block of ice. Apples and potatoes were stored in the cellar in individual bins that William built of wooden planks. The cellar walls were lined with river rock. On very hot days, it was a joy to go down into the cool cellar, where the temperature remained about 50 degrees, and we were allowed to pick out a cold, crisp apple. A trunk filled with bars of lemon soap was kept in the cellar, too.

Every day at the ranch was a new adventure for me. My brother and I could help Grandma Crissie feed the chickens. We watched the cows being milked down at the big red barn that was located across the road from the ranch house. The men who did the milking squirted milk into the cats' mouths. The milk house was really a room in the back of the ranch house that held the cream separator and the butter churn. The cream that came to the top of the milk was poured into a pitcher. The rest was taken to one of the Reno creameries, either Crescent Creamery or Chism's Creamery.

On wash day, Grandma Crissie had two very large, square washtubs, and one had lye soap in boiling water on the kitchen stove. The smell permeated the entire house, an odor that was even stronger when she gathered Uncle Bill's winter underwear and blue jeans from his room for their bi-annual washing. We could hear him bellow from upstairs, and Grandma Crissie would just laugh with a cackle.

Although Crissie was just five feet, two inches tall, she had a very high clothes line. I remember Crissie's heavy muslin sheets flapping and sailing in the Washoe Zephyrs that blew down from Peavine Peak on the way to Washoe Lake. At night, when I crawled between the sweet smelling sheets and felt the hot, flat river rock that Crissie kept in the warming oven, wrapped in old newspapers, and tied with one of her old cotton stockings, I knew I was well-loved.

My mother kept after Crissie to buy a more modern washing machine, but Grandma Crissie always said she didn't need one. Finally, one Mother's Day,

The original ranch house built by George W. Andrews in 1875, later moved about 300 feet northwest to its present site and known as the bunkhouse

Andrews Brand

GENERAL FARM SCHEDULE

Land from which crops were harvested in 1929, 140 acres – all irrigated.

All other land used for pasture in 1929, 10 acres. [Note: Crissie was renting land at that time.]

Value of farm implements and machinery used in operating this farm, including automobiles, trucks, and tractors, $890.00

(In small print, farm implements included tools, wagons, harnesses, dairy equipment, cotton gins, threshing machines, combines, apparatus for making cider, grape juice and sirup [sic] and for drying fruits.)

Amount expended in 1929 for purchase of electric light and power (paid to power company), $15.00

Amount expended *in cash* in 1929 for farm labor (exclusive of housework), $1,601.00

Farm machinery and facilities included one automobile, one truck, and one stationary gas engine.

The farm was equipped with a telephone, water was piped into the house and the bathroom, and the house was lighted by electricity.

The road adjoining the farm was an Improved D Road.

Animals born before January 1, 1930 included 5 pigs.

Cows were divided into categories:

Calves born since January 1, 1930, four.

Steers and bulls born in 1929 (yearlings), one

Heifers born in 1929 (yearlings), 10

Heifers born in 1928 and kept mainly as milk cows, eight

Cows and heifers born before 1928 and kept for milk.

The total number of cows milked during 1929 was 12, and they produced 12,045 gallons of milk. Milk sold as whole milk was 6,570 gallons, and earned $1,192.00.

In 1930, 14 cows and heifers were being milked and producing 35 gallons of milk per day.

Two cows were sold during 1929.

Spring wheat produced 10 tons from two acres.

Alfalfa cut for hay was 100 tons.

Irish or white potatoes were raised on one-half acre and produced one and one-half tons.

Fifty tons of hay and eight tons of wheat were sold.

One-eighth acre produced fruit, mostly apple trees about ten years old.

As you can see, this was not a wealthy operation, and the Depression soon brought even more hardships. When William

my mother had a washing machine delivered. It was the newest electric model with two large tubs—one that washed the clothes and the other for rinsing. These cylinders were divided by a set of wooden rollers that were turned by hand. Crissie refused to use it, and I think she was frightened by it. When my mother threatened to take it back to our home in Berkeley, California, the very next day, Crissie was very busily washing in *her* new machine.

Alum Creek ran along the west side of the Caughlin Ranch, and there were many irrigation ditches for the large fields north of the house. I remember the men turning the wheels to flood the fields in the springtime, watering the alfalfa and vegetable crops and the apple trees. Another irrigation ditch on the lower ranch ran parallel to the Truckee River. It was very deep and filled with crayfish. My brother and I would find long branches with "y" shaped twigs on the end to catch the crayfish. It was great sport to see who could get the most.

1930S ON THE RANCH

The 1930 census detailed Crissie's holdings. Frugal by nature, Crissie saved money from selling eggs, and she always seemed to have some extra money to buy more land.

DEPARTMENT OF COMMERCE – BUREAU OF THE CENSUS

FIFTEENTH CENSUS OF THE UNITED STATES: 1930 – Population

PRELIMINARY FAMILY SCHEDULE

[Based on this form, in 1930 four people lived on the ranch as follows:]

Crissie Caughlin, head of the family, age omitted, home owned, family lives on a farm. She was born in Nevada, her father was born in New Hampshire and her mother in Maine. She is listed as the proprietor and the industry as farming.

William H. Caughlin Sr. was also listed as head of the family, age 83. He was born in Australia and his mother was born in Ireland. His father's birthplace is not listed.

William H. Caughlin Jr. was 34, single and born in Nevada. He was listed as a worker on the farm and a veteran of "the World War." [World War I]

Also living on the farm was Chick Callahan, listed as a male lodger, age 25. A native of Nevada, his father was born in California and his mother was born in Nevada.

Joe Rondo, ranch hand who was more like family

haps when we become a famous "Dude Ranch" you will get out here... You know we have a graveled and paved highway now through to San Francisco, and they expect to keep the road open all winter.... There is talk of Smith Valley or Lyon County not being able to go on with their schools after New Years, as so much of the funds are tied up in the banks, but I think they will manage somehow to go on! It would be hard for our boys, for we couldn't send them away this year! Suppose you got a little storm this week, as we did! We had about 3 inches of snow here in the Valley with more higher up, they say....

                     Lovingly,
                     Alice Hunewill
                     (daughter-in-law of
                     Esther)

Simpson, Nev.
Jan. 8th, 1933

My Dear Crissie;

    Your letter was received a day or two ago, and I, with all the family concurring, think you are the most *generous* and *unselfish* person I know of anywhere! To offer to take in the whole "H" family, and help us out in this strenuous and trying time! It is just like your own dear self, and we thoroughly appreciate the offer. I can assure you, however, though we did not know surely whether or not school was to open until the "bus" came around Monday a.m., it *did* open and I suppose will at least run this next semester. The county is pretty hard up, as is the whole of Nevada now, but I suppose things will straighten out after awhile. Suppose you heard the report of the Minden Bank being closed last week; Stanley was out to Minden yesterday, and it seems the radio broadcast was for Minden, Gardnerville, I believe it was, and Mr. Wanhold said if all the deposits were all drawn out, there would still be a surplus of over $100,000, so that bank will rate better than ever!... Once again I want to thank you, Crissie dear, for your generous thoughtfulness, and may 1933 be a prosperous and pleasant year for you and yours.

                     Best Wishes,
                     Lovingly,
                     Alice Huniwell

Joe Rondo, a painting by Shiela Lonie

JOE RONDO

Crissie depended primarily on one ranch hand, Joe Rondo. Joe was a quiet, hard-working man, who was treated as

died on January 16, 1932, Crissie was left alone with Bill Jr. and several hired hands to help her operate the ranch. Uncle Bill was a "fixture" at the ranch. Badly shell shocked from World War I, he was in very sad shape his entire life. He did help Crissie by chopping wood, mending fences, hunting deer, and fishing.

Crissie could no longer afford to be a lady of leisure, as some neighbors once viewed her. Now, she seldom left the ranch. Pillow cases were patched with material from flower sacks and lace to make them look new. Aprons were made from old dresses. Letters from the Hunewills in Bridgeport, California, described the impact of Nevada's bank closures on ranchers.

[year unknown]
Bridgeport, March 20

My dear Niece,
.... Times are not the best in this part of the country. Everybody is failing and going through the bankruptcy law to pay their debts....
From your
Aunt Esther

Bridgeport Ranch
December 4th, 1932

My Dear Crissie;
As I have now "more time than money," I've really gotten around to write to you! How are you all this glorious weather! We can at least be glad for the sunshine and health, even if the banks are all closed. It didn't affect us much, as what few pennies we did have were in the Minden Bank, (Farmers' Bank of Carson Valley) and they are all right. I sincerely hope and suppose that you were banking in the Kirman Bank, which of course, was all right.

It surely was a terrible blow for Nevada, wasn't it? With all the taxes just due everywhere, and so much school money tied up, too! Most people around here are affected by it, but most all are hoping that they will make some arrangement and reopen soon. Weren't you surprised at the Democratic "landslide?" I thought it would be a close run, but nothing like it was. Well, we think things are at the bottom of the scale now and that there must be an upward trend very soon! We are not pessimistic (and I know you are not), and we'll all come out smiling in the spring, "Smilin' through...."

I wish you and yours would ever come out here to see us, so we could repay some of our many obligations! Per-

Bill, Syrene, Rowland, and Betsy in a sleigh being pulled by their dog Bob

Ned and Rose Grove, Bill Caughlin (behind Rose), Syrene, Betsy, Rowland and William Caughlin standing by a gate at the ranch, c. 1910

Horse and buggy taking children to school

Crissie feeding chickens at the ranch, March 1908

Group on the big rock, Bill Caughlin, Minnie Collins, Lena Bryan, Crissie, Rowland, sitting on the rock is Syrene and Betsy with Vernice Collins.

Dr. Billingsley, Joe Rondo and Bill Caughlin

a member of the family. Born in Mexico, by the age of 10 he lived in the Monterey and San Francisco areas where he received his education at the missions. He was a well-read man and the only hired hand that ate meals with the family and had his own special chair at the table.

It amazed me to learn that he had a violent past and had served time in the Nevada State Prison for murder. The story our family believed was that Joe got drunk in a Reno bar on a Saturday night and killed a German man for insulting the American flag. After his parole, none of the other ranchers would hire him except Crissie.

I found a slightly different story in the Nevada state prison records. The jury could not reach a verdict in the first trial, but at Joe's second trial, the jury returned a guilty verdict in less than an hour—"Guilty of Murder in the Second Degree," December 29, 1917. Joe was sentenced to not less than one or more than 13 years. The court documents read:

> In the opinion of the writer the facts in this case disclose an absolute, unprovoked killing on the part of the defendant of old Jake Himmelberger, an old character who has been about this city for twenty-seven years, working at different employments, and who had the reputation of being very harmless, but quite loquacious while drinking.
>
> The defendant, Joe Rondo, is an old "Buckaroo" and cowboy, who has worked for all of the large cattlemen and ranch owners of the Western part of this county, of which he has been a resident for approximately forty years.
>
> On the night of the alleged offense of which the defendant was convicted it appears that he had been drinking and that he met Himmelberger, the deceased, in the Star Barrel House saloon at about three o'clock on the morning in question; that they had a few drinks together and were sitting talking at a table in the saloon when the deceased, who was very drunk, stood up and told Rondo not to call him a Dane, and then staggered over the chair in which Rondo was sitting and laid his hand on Rondo's shoulder in a drunken manner. Instantly Rondo jumped to his feet, told the deceased to get away from him or he would kill him, and that the deceased staggered away from the defendant in the opposite direction, walking up toward the bar; that a minute, perhaps, elapsed between the time the defendant first flashed the gun until the bystanders told him to put the gun up, not paying any particular attention to him, because of the fact that Himmelberger was so drunk and the men knew one another, that they did not think anything was going to happen. A minute later, however, the defendant again flourished the gun while the deceased was several

feet from him, standing in a stooping position due to his drunken condition, and defendant shouted "I will kill you, you son-of-a-bitch" and the deceased simply said "Shoot." The defendant fired one shot, which killed Himmelberger almost instantly.

The defendant took the stand at the trial and stated that Himmelberger had said something derogatory to the American Flag, and repeatedly talked in this manner concerning the United States, and that he had shot him because he feared he was going to do him great bodily harm and that at one time during the conversation the deceased, he said, shoved the table against him. All of these matters were denied by spectators, one reliable witness, a plasterer by trade, (who happened in the saloon about half an hour before the shooting occurred while on his way to work) was sitting at the same table at which these men were talking, and he denied absolutely that any remarks were made concerning the American flag, or that any violence or offer of violence was made by the deceased toward the defendant.

As a matter of fact, in the opinion of the writer [district attorney], the defendant, out of a spirit of malice and without any provocation whatever, deliberately killed Jake Himmelberger, making the offense clearly one of murder in the second degree.

Owing to the fact that the defendant has lived in this community for over forty years, and, in so far as the same has been discussed, has always borne a reputation for peace and quietness, and is a man seventy-four years of age, small of physique, I think the jury in the first case failed to convict purely through motives of sympathy;...[4]

Joe served about five and a half years in the state prison, mostly as a trustee who worked on the prison farm and surrounding farms as far away as Fernley, Fallon, and Lake Tahoe. Crissie and Betsy often took food to the prison for a picnic with Joe on visiting day. When he was paroled on November 15, 1923, he returned to Crissie's ranch. He still went to the bar every week. Every Saturday night, he sold Crissie's dog Skidoo to get money for drinks. However, the dog never stayed sold and always beat Joe back to the ranch.

Crissie always said Joe saved her life. One night, William arrived home drunk, demanding that he be allowed to sell the ranch for $10,000. When Crissie opposed him, he pulled out a gun and started toward her. Joe interceded and took the gun from William.

Joe helped Crissie for about 10 years after William's death. He adored Crissie; he admired her intelligence, and the two talked to each other about a wide range of subjects from litera

Syrene Caughlin with geese near the big rock, c. 1910

Four children feeding chickens and geese at the ranch, c. 1905

ture, like Shakespeare and Mark Twain, to the best methods for operating the ranch. Each year on December 21 or 22, Crissie held a birthday dinner for Joe and invited all the family. Crissie recounted the final days of Joe's life in her diary.

August 29, 1942 – Loaned Joe $1.
September 1, 1942 – Joe in hospital three days, too much booze again.
September 4, 1942 – Joe quite ill—gave me $5.
September 5, 1942 – Betsy tried to get Joe to the hospital. 4 p.m. called Sheriff. They came and took Joe to the hospital.
September 6, 1942 – Went to see Joe. Nearly gone. Died 4 p.m. Called priest. age 97.
September 9, 1942 – Buried Joe in Mission Delores Cemetery, grave side services.

Crissie noted just the facts, without mentioning any personal feelings. I can't help but think the loss of her good friend affected Crissie deeply. In fact, she made special arrangements for his burial at the Mission Delores Cemetery in California, where he received his education. Also, Crissie made no comment on one irony; he died on her birthday.

NEAREST NEIGHBORS

The Caughlin's nearest neighbors lived kitty-corner across the old Verdi Road, to the northwest. The Schiappacasse's (pronounced shep-case) had four children—Johnny, Mike, Laura and Alma. Johnny and Mike were friends with Bill Jr., and Crissie's diary mentions their hunting and fishing trips. My mother and Aunt Betsy were friends with the older girls. In recent years, I had a wonderful opportunity to talk to the youngest girl, now Alma Westegard. She remembered some good "gossip" about Crissie.

> Your Grandpa Bill was always good to your Grandma Crissie. She led a *real good* life when they got married. In fact, I guess all the farm women kind of envied Crissie, because she had such an easy life and had such nice clothes and had somebody to cook for her. [I remember a Chinaman named Que was the cook. Syrene and Betsy couldn't go into the kitchen, because he would chase them out with a meat clever.]
>
> He told the men who worked for him when to have her horse and buggy ready for her. She used to go down to the Century Club and play cards (bridge or canasta). She always had nice clothes—he saw to it she had nice clothes. Your grandfather was also strict. One time Syrene and Betsy were going to school and had lipstick on. He got a dishrag and washed it off of them.
>
> Later on, Crissie took the ranch over and she did all the work. When William died, first Crissie rented out the whole ranch, but then she decided to run it herself. My mother asked, "Do you think you will do well if you operate it yourself?"
>
> Crissie said, "Oh, I know I can."

She really *did work!* Then she didn't go down and play cards, because she had to stay there and run the ranch. She did all the cooking and all the work. Joe Rondo worked for her, but she always decided everything. Curly milked for her, and he married [Hazel Murphy, a girl Crissie took in and raised, who also worked for her a few years. Crissie never did her own milking.] Johnny and Mike helped her with the haying, but toward the end, she did her own milking and fed the chickens and pigs.

It was unusual for women to run ranches at that time, and nobody had as much land as your grandmother. Most people would have 20 to 50 acres. Around where Nixon Avenue is now used to be all small farms and they had water rights. She always had good water rights because your Great Grandfather Andrews helped build the Last Chance or Steamboat Ditch. He was an engineer.

It was always fun to go up to Crissie's house and talk to her. She always talked to me, and sometimes she gave me a piece of cake. She encouraged me to go to the university, and I was the only one in our family to attend college and become a teacher.

She told me, "If you come over to my house and dust for me, I'll give you 25 cents a day." That was like $25 today. So I would take all the books out of her bookcase and dust them, and I dusted the buffet and fiddled around on the piano. Crissie would sing and whistle for me. She was real proud of you [Shiela] for going to New York to study music.

She was not a very big woman, and she had gray hair pulled back in a knot. Then later, when permanents came out, your Grandma Crissie would get a permanent all the time.[5]

As a child, I remember going to Schiappacasse's to play. Alma's mother kept butter and soda crackers in their cellar. Kids were allowed to eat all they wanted, and it tasted so good on a hot day. We also could also pick fresh strawberries.

When I was first married, Crissie insisted that my new husband and I go see Mrs. Schiappacasse, because she had a wedding present for us. Bob and I walked over to their house on the dirt road. Alma, Laura, and their mother gave us a chenille bedspread with flowers all over it, and we used that for years. Mrs. Schiappacasse was so excited about our visit that she brought up some of her deceased husband's homemade wine, and I think it was about 110 proof!

Alma's niece, Prilla Fordham, joined me when I talked to Alma, and she remembered the haying operation well enough to describe it. The workers would arrive at a haystack with a wagonload of hay and pull up to a Jackson hayfork. The huge

William Caughlin in horse and buggy, with Crissie;s sulky in the barn, which was lost when the barn burned down, c. 1932

Front row, Rowland, Besy and Syrene at the ranch with unidentified ranch hands

Crissie's trunk and rocking chair

Crissie's pickle jar (left) and Bower's canister with ABS initials on the base

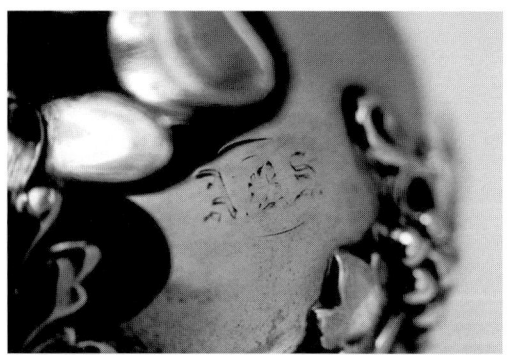

fork was on a derrick and was operated with pulleys and cables. On one end of the cable was the fork, and at the other end, horses moved back and forth, which moved the fork from the hay wagon to the haystack in the field. The haystack had to be built just right, with a rounded top, so that rain and snow would run off and not stay on the hay.

THE WAR YEARS

Neighbors viewed the Caughlin's as prosperous and Crissie, a lady of leisure who had a Chinese cook and time to attend meetings of several women's clubs, according to Alma Schiappacasse. The truth is that Crissie's life only looked easy, because she had a wonderful sense of humor and many friends, so she often left the house to visit others.

My father, Edward Seagrave, helped Crissie by selling topsoil during World War II, but Crissie really would not let anyone else run her ranch. There was never any question as to who was in
charge of the ranch. In some of her letters during the war years, she discussed the ranch business with her daughters. Most were addressed to "My Dear Betsy" and signed, "Love, Mother." She also included news of Reno, war shortages, and union strikes.

Wednesday, June 3, 1942
Dear Sis (nickname for Syrene),

I am going to Homemakers this afternoon and have my car serviced while I am there.... Frank has five or six Japs weeding onions, pays 50 cents per hour, but all the Italians are using them, so I'm not saying anything.[6] If there is dirty work, they will soon find out and that will end it.

Sunday, August 5, 1944

I'm out on the porch and the wind is quite strong, but in my corner it is nice. The planes are sure going—about 8:30 this a.m. there was a formation going north of about 15 planes. They looked beautiful. Imagine 1,000 of them. Bill said they were bombers. They did not make much noise; they were pretty high.

Min and I may go up to the Lake for a few days.[7] The Farm Bureau has a camp where we can go the last part of August. We pay 65 cents per day for electricity; come on up....

Thursday, March 29, 1945

.... The real estate man just left and thinks he has a buy for Commercial Row. He wants it for $6,000. Well, I just thought, "Take it and get rid of it." I've paid a lot of money for taxes and still eating, and next year it will be more.... I presume whoever gets it will sell for double, but I would never put up a building there unless I fell into something I know nothing of....

A funny thing happened yesterday. I went out and got my car, parked it in front of the door. I saw a man walking around the barn. He saw me and came and got into his car. I thought it was someone looking at the Lake Ditch, so I went in and got ready and they were *still* there.... I found out he had taken a wheel off the binder and was trying to get the other one off and chains and had them in his car. Louis was out plowing and thought he would go see what he was doing. He made the fellow put them back, and who do you think it was? The game warden.... so you see it is not safe to go away and leave the place alone.

Friday, September 21, 1945

It is so miserable out this a.m.; I don't feel like doing a thing.... I've got a lot of peaches to cook, got my pears and tomatoes put up, my coal and wood in and wheat for winter....

January 16, 1946

.... The Martin's home across the street went for $35,000. The old Washoe County Bank building is to be torn down and a five-story building put up there. I'm glad the New Village [shopping center on California Street, Reno] down the road is progressing. I won't have so far to go shopping. I understand they are to have stores, etc., so the people won't have to go to Reno.

Have you any trouble getting butter and other groceries? We haven't had any trouble as yet. It is hard to get butter. I'm supposed to get a pound today. I got a jar of Miracle Whip Saturday [referring to food shortages following the war].

February 7, 1946
    The planning board has been looking for a truck lane, to have a route just for them, to start this side of Lawton Springs, go as near the railroad track as they can.... come into Highway 40 and on east. There is too much traffic on Fourth Street going east. I hope they don't decide to go through our place.
    .... There is a movement on foot to purchase Bowers Mansion for $100,000. I told them, see Harolds Club. He might help. He has just given the YWCA $10,000 to pay off their mortgage and put an annex....

Thursday, March 21, 1946
    Your wonderful and newsy letter reached me Monday.... I just sat down to answer when Mrs. Scheps came over after some eggs to set.... I'm trying to sew a bit, making aprons out of old dresses, etc. Apron goods will soon be on the market and then I can have some real good ones.... I did not have to pay income [tax] this year. I'm going to get some flowers for my old hat and wear it again. I'll have a brown and also a blue outfit this spring. Now I'm going to finish my dishes. I'm cooking beans for tonight.... [typical Crissie letter]

Monday, April 29, 1946
    .... Don't look for me on Mother's Day. I can't see my way clear. The water in the Last Chance Ditch has been out for three or four days, a bad break just across Hunter Creek. The company has had a big shovel up there and tearing the side hill down, making a new part there. I just see some of the big trucks going down. Hope they are through....
    Lizzie Scolari has sold her ranch and the Hunter Creek Dairy, so I suppose there will be another town up there, as the Brown Motel (same people that promoted Rhodes Ranch) has taken it over. I can sit on the front porch and watch the procession.

Friday, May 31, 1946
    I bought some wheat for my chicks today at 4 ½ cents per pound. Two sacks came to $11, but I've sold that many eggs to pay for it. I hope it lasts me through the season, for all the wheat has been taken over, and you can't buy a bit from the warehouses. Louis said this a.m. eggs were going up to $3 per dozen. I had better be putting some in crocks for winter. It is not more than two months ago when the radio advised everyone to sell their chickens. I'm going to have a chicken dinner for Minerva's birthday. She has all her rooms rented and they do their own work. I haven't told her yet, I am making my house over in apartments, but I think it will pay me, as several have spoken for them, even if I don't rent it in the winter. [Housing shortage with GI's returning from war.]

Saturday, June 29, 1946

.... Minerva would like to have you get some stockings for her. She only has one pair of nylons. She can't get them here. She wears 8 ½ and would like 54 gauge. I said you had to get what you could.... Minerva won't care if you get three or four pair. I have seven pair with those you sent, but believe me, I keep them under cover. She paid $12 per yard for silk print enough to make a dress. Cost her $50, and here I'm wearing any old thing.... People can't find places to stay. If I was very energetic, I'd fix my rooms and make $5 a night, but I just can't.

April 16, 1947

.... The plumbers are on a strike since April 7.... Your men have certainly got the right idea these times in converting old or roomy homes into smaller quarters for anyone who needs a small apartment. That makes me think of my old ranch house, and also makes me think of a couple of fellows here last week that wanted to put a new roof on the house and fix these back windows so they won't leak, and *guaranteed* it, mind you; $506, furnish everything. I could hardly get rid of them, when I happened to think of Roger [Donnelly]. I told them my son-in-law offered to bring his men up here and do the job for a vacation. Oh no! They could not do that. They would not have the material etc. "Why," I told them, "he would bring all the necessary equipment on one of his big trucks and have a fine vacation." Well, they thought that was not the right thing, to have Californians come in here and not patronize home industry. We certainly had to match wits. I haven't heard from them since.

April 25, 1947

The review of the Sharons brought old memories. Once upon a time, when I was in my early teens, Will Sharon used to come down to Reno to the dances. Well, I met him and we danced and had quite a case. We corresponded for about two years.... He left Virginia [City] and our writing ceased.

May 4, 1947

.... The unions have certainly been raising havoc in this county. I don't know whether I can get the shingles [for the roof] or not. Sy thinks by the last of May this strike will be over, but it has been running for some time. I saw Holgate last night, the engineer of the planning board, so I can get the permit. The Bonanza Club wanted to do some alterations and went at it without consulting the board and was sued for $30,000. I told Holgate, Roger was going to do the work, and he was not certain if he could come out of another state and do the work, but said, "Take a chance."

We did not have a hoist before. Bill and Joe Callahan packed them [shingles] up stairs to the closet and they hoisted them up through the manhole, which would be much cheaper—if I can get a man to help Bill. Men don't want to work any more.

May 26, 1949
　… one night bout three or four weeks ago, about midnight, a loud clap of thunder, a flash of lightening and an earthquake all occurred at the same time. Wasn't that a surprise. I never, in my short span, witnessed or felt that combination.

CHAPTER NINE
Caughlin Ranch Celebrities

ALMOST EVERYONE CRISSIE MET soon became a friend of the family, and the Caughlin Ranch served as a retreat for many of them, during good times and bad. Crissie loved to entertain and among her family, friends, and guests were some names that are well known in Nevada history.

MARY STODDARD DOTEN

Alfred Doten, Virginia City newspaperman, whose journal chronicled the Comstock boom, mentioned Crissie and her brother Benjamin several times, noting when they sang for social events or attended dances. Mrs. Bettie Andrews was considered a "Doten family friend," and she was especially close to Doten's wife, Mary Stoddard Doten. Mary came to Virginia City from Camden, New York, to teach school. At first, she stayed with her Aunt Lucy Batterman, whose husband was the superintendent of the Gould and Curry Mines. Mary taught at the Gold Hill School from 1872 to 1874.

She and Doten were married in 1873, while George and Bettie still lived in Washoe City. Two years later, Mary sent for her small daughter Milly and her mother Sarah Stoddard. Mary and Alf had four children together, but because Doten spent much of his money and time on alcohol and friends, Mary returned to teaching in 1884. She moved herself and her five children to Reno where she taught at Reno High School. Crissie and Milly Doten were friends.

The parallels in Mary Doten's and Bettie Andrews' lives are striking. Both had alcoholic husbands, and both raised small children and earned an income with little help from their husbands. Both suffered the loss of children—Bettie lost the twins as babies and Ben as a young adult. Mary lost two grown daughters, one to typhoid and one to suicide.

Beyond that, their similarities ended. Mary Doten returned to her teaching career and was active in Nevada education, the women's suffrage movement, and civic organizations. She spoke at the 20th Century Club, one of the women's organizations that Crissie joined later.[1] In contrast, Bettie managed the ranch operations, with the help of her children, but she was not involved in women's clubs or the suffrage movement.

Mary Doten, schoolteacher and pioneer educator in Nevada

Kate Caughlin Grove (William Caughlin's sister) married Dr. Wixom and became the stepmother of Emma Nevada

EMMA WIXOM NEVADA

Crissie was always proud of our family's connection by marriage to 19th century opera star Emma Nevada. Emma was born to Dr. and Mrs. William W. Wixom at the Alpha mining camp, near Nevada City, California, in 1859. As a child of 4, wrapped in an American flag, Emma sang the "Star Spangled Banner" for miners. Shortly after that in 1863 or 1864, Dr. Wixom moved his family to Austin, Nevada, where Emma was raised. When Emma was 13, her mother died, and Emma was sent back to California to finish her education at Mills College, a young women's seminary.

Emma Nevada

In 1877, she sailed for Hamburg to study opera, but found herself in a predicament when tour leader Dr. Adrian Ebell died. The other young singers returned to the states, but Emma was determined to stay and study voice, which she did with the famous operatic teacher Madame Marchessi.

While Emma was in Europe, her father married Kate Caughlin, sister of William Caughlin, in December 1879 at Elko, Nevada. Five months later, Emma sang as Emma Nevada (selecting the name that was both the California county of her birth and her home state) for the Queen of England. The queen presented Emma with a gift—a valuable diamond necklace. The royal recognition opened many doors for Emma, and she toured throughout Europe over the next five years.

In 1885, Emma Nevada toured the United States, taking the opportunity to perform at Piper's Opera House in Virginia City and at the Methodist Church in Austin, Nevada. It was her only return to Nevada.[3]

There is no record of Crissie attending the Emma Nevada concert in Virginia City. Emma was six years older than Crissie, and her fame in Europe was growing at the same time that Crissie and her brother Ben were singing at Nevada events. It was a full 10 years later that Crissie became related to Emma, when Crissie married William Caughlin. Although time and distance stood between the two, Crissie forever considered Emma Nevada to be "family," and they shared a love of singing.

Emma died in June of 1940 in Liverpool, England, fifteen years before Crissie's death. When Grandma Crissie talked about her, I could tell she was enamored of Emma. Crissie took me to Virginia City to show me Emma's trunk and the costumes that were stored at Piper's Opera House. No letters from Emma survived, but I have always believed there must have been a personal connection between the two, because Emma left her opera glasses to Crissie. Crissie gave them to me when I attended my first opera in San Francisco.

JEFFRIES-JOHNSON, HEAVYWEIGHT CHAMPS

Independence Day 1910 brought national attention to Reno with the championship-boxing match between the first black heavyweight titleholder Jack Johnson and former titleholder Jim Jeffries, a retired boxer who was white. Jeffries was referred to as "the Great White Hope" or the "chosen representative of the white race," according to author Jack London.[4] The fight brought the world to Reno. Still just a town with a little more than 10,000 citizens, Renoites watched as 22,000 people—double the Reno population—inundated the town to view the battle between the races.

> "Every hotel room in town was taken, and miles of special trains with sleeping cars lined the tracks," Robert Laxalt wrote in his history of Nevada. "Betting activity was feverish. The temper of the crowds was downright dangerous, not only because Jack Johnson was a black, but because he had committed what was then regarded as a scandalous indiscretion. He was living openly at his training camp with a white wife."[5]

That training camp was Rick's Resort on South Verdi Road, now Mayberry Drive. It was located on property that was at one time a Caughlin Ranch meadow.[6] Rick's was really a roadhouse, and there were "girls" or prostitutes upstairs, but no one in the neighborhood acknowledged them. My Aunt Betsy was a child at the time, and she told me about hiding in a wagon so she could go with her father to watch the sparring at Rick's Resort.

Clara Crisles of Carson City and Crissie Caughlin of Reno at a tea held to raise funds for the Bowers' Mansion at the home of Mrs. John Davidson, Sept. 1944. Persia Bowers was a childhood friend of Crissie's

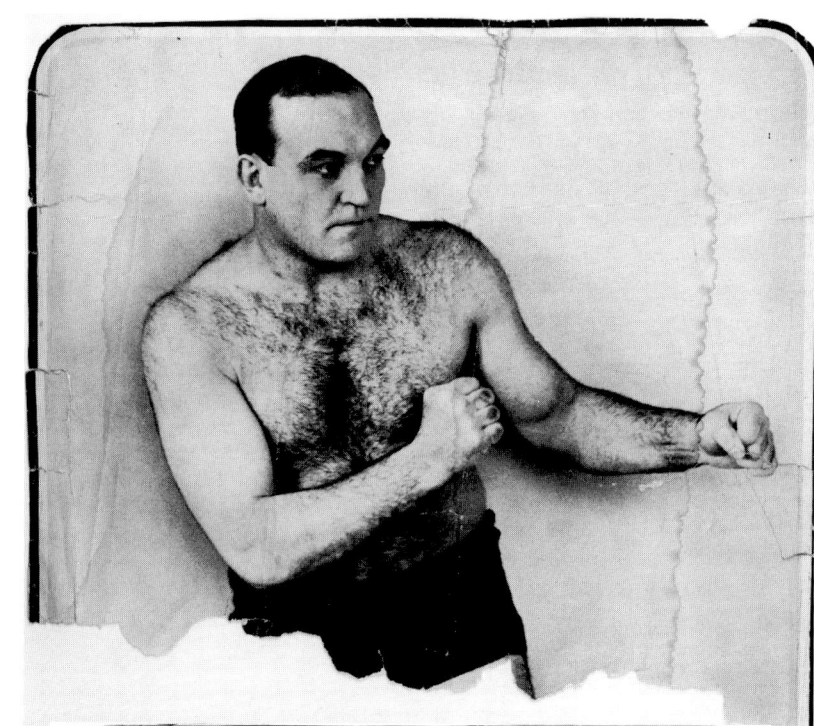

Posters for the Johnson-Jefferies fight

Crissie and Max Baer, c. 1930

Johnson's camp could only be reached by automobile or horse. He welcomed the fans and put on a show. He would joke as he dueled with his sparring partner, Kid Cotton. He would invite the fans to have a few drinks, play some poker and listen to a jazz band he had hired.[7]

At a time when many people still worked twelve hours to earn $1, fans paid $30 for an "Inner Circle" seat to the Jeffries-Johnson fight.[8]

Crissie's friend, Laura Tucker, took a photo of Johnson and his sparring partner on the ranch property, proof enough that Crissie was interested in the event and may have been in the audience.

Women, not usually allowed at such sporting events, were provided for in a unique manner. A separate section closed off at the sides was constructed for them so they could enjoy the spectacle and not be seen by others, but many members of the fair sex, including Johnson's white wife, sat in the audience that day.[9]

Johnson won the fight in 15 rounds, a victory that stunned the crowd into a funeral-like silence. While Reno saw no violence from the fight, other cities across the nation reported race riots and deaths. My grandfather attended the fight and saved a rare program and large pictures of both fighters that listed their fight statistics.

MAX BAER

Johnson was not the only fighter Crissie met in her lifetime. One-time heavyweight champion Max Baer fought from 1929 through 1941, and Crissie had her photograph taken with him. Like Johnson, he worked out on Verdi Road in front of the ranch house. However, since he fought in Reno more than once, I don't know what year the photograph was taken.

Photo from the famous Jeffries and Johnson fight of 1910. Johnson trained at Rick's Resort near the Caughlin Ranch

Max Baer with Gloria Rupper, Indian foster child raised by Crissie and Dolly, who worked for Crissie in her home. Taken on the South Verdi Road in front of the Caughlin Ranch house

Photo identified as Will James by Betsy Caughlin Donnelly. James was a friend of Bill Caughlin's and lived at the ranch for a few months

Will James did two drawings for Crissie when he was staying at the ranch, self portrait

Alice James, wife's portrait

WILL JAMES, AUTHOR AND ARTIST

Although much has been written about Will James and his years spent in Nevada, few people realize that he lived at the Caughlin Ranch for a short time. Author Anthony Amaral publicized James's connection to the Caughlin Ranch.

> "While James was away, Alice decided to find a place where she and James could live and which would allow her husband more room for his work. Her brother, Paul, heard of a studio apartment for rent west of Reno on the Coughlin [sic] ranch located on a hillside with acres of rolling sagebrush. When he took her there, Alice knew this would be a place for them. She wasn't certain what James's reaction would be. Money was still scarce although the *Sunset* assignments and a few commercial art jobs for local businesses had helped. But she felt a studio for James would be an encouragement.
>
> After James returned and Alice showed him their new home with his own studio, he was ecstatic. It would cause a pinch, he admitted, but was worth it all. They never felt that pinch, as the ranch owner agreed to lower the rent in exchange for James attending to a few daily chores on the ranch."[10]

Amaral dated the time as the summer of 1922. Crissie told me that Will James lived alone, not with Alice, and Crissie let him stay rent-free in a shack at Jap Flats, near present-day McCarran Boulevard and Plumb Lane. He ate at the ranch house and became friends with my Uncle Bill. At one time, the family owned a sawhorse that was made for Bill and had James' initials carved on it. He drew pictures for Crissie that she just tacked to the wall. One is a self-portrait and the other is a portrait of Alice on a bucking horse—a rare sight in those days to have a woman on a bucking horse. Crissie had an early photo of him, and neither the photo nor the drawings he did for Crissie have been published before this.

> "One day in 1923 he sat down in the little apartment they were then renting on a ranch outside of Reno and dashed off an illustrated story called "Bucking Horses and Bucking-Horse Riders," which he sent to *Scribner's Magazine*. He confided to Alice that it was "too easy done to be any good" and that when it was rejected he would never again try writing. It was, however, accepted promptly, and James was paid a handsome fee.... He worked all day at his drawing board and desk, rolling Bull Durham cigarettes and refusing to call it quits until dinnertime. He quickly sold another story to *Scribner's*, another to the *Saturday Evening Post* and a three-part series to *Sunset*. Soon famed editor Maxwell Perkins was writing to him to say that Scribner's publishing house would bring out James' collected stories as *Cowboys North and South*.[11]

The Caughlin Ranch may have given James the time and space he needed to meld his two talents. The resulting financial success made it possible for Will and Alice James to purchase his first car, a 1920 Pierce Arrow, and a parcel of land in Washoe Valley. The cabin Alice's father and brothers built for them still stands at Foresta Institute. The home sits at the base of the Sierra looking east across Franktown Road and Washoe Valley.

Earlier, James spent time in a Nevada prison on charges of stealing cattle just outside of Ely, Nevada, in Utah. His pardon, based on his before-and-after drawing of himself showing how he was reformed by his prison time, is one of the better-known Nevada stories of Will James. He also drew the first Reno Rodeo program cover.

James' horse named Happy—the one that bucked him off and knocked him unconscious—his recovery at a friend's home where he met Alice, his wild antics performed during the time when alcohol took over his life, his real identity—discovered only after his death—all of these stories are more familiar than that time spent living and writing at the Caughlin Ranch.

LORENZO LATIMER, ARTIST

Crissie's talents were many—businesswoman, singer, whistler, hostess, chef, mother, grandmother—but her children's talents were in the arts. No doubt these were passed down from Crissie's father George, who taught penmanship and drew beautifully—talents he did not pursue. Both my mother and Aunt Betsy loved painting. A young schoolteacher, Dora Groesbeck, who stayed at the Caughlin Ranch for a time and became one of Crissie's friends, nurtured

"Truckee River" by Syrene Caughlin. Done as part of Lorenzo Latimer's class.

Fallen Leaf Lake by Lorenzo Latimer

Dog Valley by Lorenzo Latimer

Autumn in Reno by Lorenzo Latimer

Lorenzo P. Latimer, Oct. 22, 1925

Dora Groesbeck, nee Navacovich, art teacher at Sparks High School who brought Lorenzo P. Latimer to Reno to teach watercolor classes, c. 1916

Dora Groesbeck

Dora Groesbeck and Al Caughlin at her house on Mill Street, Reno

their artistic talents. Dora brought the famous California artist, Lorenzo Latimer, to Reno where he taught his wonderful plein-air watercolor technique to young ladies. My mother and Aunt Betsy were among Latimer's students, and I have several Latimer watercolors and some of my mother's and Betsy's watercolors.

LORENZO LATIMER FUNERAL SET ON COAST

Lorenzo P. Latimer, eighty-five year old noted California artist, who was well known in Reno, died Tuesday night of a heart attack at a hospital in Berkeley.

For more than twenty years he made annual sketching trips to Reno to paint scenes of Nevada. He founded the Latimer Art Club, composed of Nevada artists, and the first art club to be formed in the state.

From 1893 to 1905, Latimer conducted art classes in San Francisco and at Fallen Leaf Lake in the Lake Tahoe region. In 1916 he began sketching tours in Reno.... to do homage with his brush to the Nevada desert and to the beauty of the autumn scenery around Reno.

He had been painting at Fallen Leaf Lake in the Tahoe region and was persuaded to form a class in Reno through the efforts of Mrs. Nevada Wilson Riley and Mrs. Dora N. Groesbeck, who had studied with him.

In 1921, the Latimer Art Club of Nevada was officially organized in Reno with Mrs. Minerva Pierce as its first president. It is still in existence and the members periodically hold exhibitions.[11]

The first retrospective exhibit was shown from April through July 2004 at Reno's Museum of Art.

CHAPTER TEN
Crissie's Battle for Water Rights

IN THE DESERT, water can mean life or death, especially for ranchers. In the Truckee Meadows, the configuration of creeks and water ditches has changed over the years, but in 1881, *Thompson and West* described the system of irrigation canals, including the Last Chance Ditch engineered by Crissie's father:

> The South Side Canal takes water one mile below Mayberry's, and carries it to Wheeler's ranch, five miles south of Reno.... Commencing two miles above Hunter's Bridge, and running around the hills, a distance of thirteen miles towards Steamboat Springs, is the Last Chance Ditch. It was built by farmers in 1876, and cost $15,000.[1]

Crissie proudly told me of her battle to retain the ranch's water rights—rights her father earned when he engineered and helped build the Last Chance Ditch. She saved the story of her battle in newspaper clippings, which uncharacteristically for Crissie, were not identified by publication or date.[2] It appears that Crissie confirmed her water rights as early as 1913, but in the mid-1930s a court battle developed that lasted three years and went all the way to the Nevada Supreme Court where her water rights were upheld.

Basically, as I understand the story, various properties along the Last Chance Ditch had been sold over the years before the ditch ended up in receivership to the United Nevada Bank as part of the Holcomb estate. At that point, the Nevada Public Service Commission decided to charge an equal fee to all ditch users. However, several of the original ranchers still owned water rights as part of their deeds, and they decided to fight. Crissie and others filed their lawsuit in 1935, according to these newspaper clippings.

[letterhead, State of Nevada Engineer's Office, Carson City]
March 29th, 1913

Dear Mrs. Caughlin:--
    I have your letter of the 28th. inst., requesting a copy of the Proof of Appropriation filed in the year 1909.

Alum Creek at Mayberry, the Last Chance Ditch flume, lower Caughlin Ranch

I am enclosing herewith the copy of the original, which is on file here.

I was disappointed in the Government instituting the suit now pending as it was the intention of the office to get at the compilation of these proofs of appropriation as soon as possible to settle the rights under the state law. It will be made as inexpensive as possible I am told, and the Government does not intend to contest the rights, but merely define them.

Trusting that this meets your request, I am,

Very truly yours,
Wm. Kearney

DISTRICT OF NEVADA, SS.

The PRESIDENT of the United States of America.

To Orr Water Ditch Company, Steamboat Canal Company, Orr Extension Ditch Company, Spanish Springs Valley Ditch Company, North Truckee Ditch Company, South Side Irrigating Canal Company, D.C. Wheeler, Incorporated, Scott Ranch Ditch Company, Glendale Irrigation Ditch Company, Riverside Mill Company, Wadsworth Light and Power Company, Verdi Lumber Company, Washoe County Bank, Wells Estate Company, Scheeline Banking and Trust Company, Humphrey Supply Company, Washoe Lake Reservoir and Galena Creek Ditch Company, Reno Development Company, Robert Steele Corporation, Reno Power Light and Water Company, the Truckee River General Electric Company,

Each and all of the above being corporations. [This was followed by a list of names including C. Caughlin and a number of other well-known Nevada names such as three Avansinos, B. Capurro, William Holcomb, A. Kietzke, P.A. McCarran, George Peckham, B. Raggio, J.O. Sessions, A. Semenza....] GREETING:

You are hereby commanded that you and each of you, personally appear before the Judge of our District Court of the United States for the District of Nevada, at the courtroom of said court in Carson City, Nevada, on the 25th day March 1913, to answer unto a bill of complaint exhibited against you in said court by UNITED STATES OF AMERICA: and to do further and receive whatever said court shall have considered in behalf; and this you are not to omit under the penalty of Two Hundred and Fifty Dollars.

Samuel Platt
United States Attorney for the State of Nevada

Memorandum: - The defendants are to file their answer or other defense, in the above mentioned suit, in the clerk's office at Carson City, Nevada, on or before the twentieth day after service, excluding the day thereof; otherwise the bill may be taken pro confesso.

Newspaper articles credited Crissie's father, George W. Andrews, with building eight miles of the Last Chance Ditch, which is confusing, because Crissie always said that he was involved in building the Steamboat Ditch. Whatever his actual role, I believe his part in building the ditch system is one of his legacies to the Truckee Meadows.

> LAST CHANCE DITCH
> Last Chance Ditch Case
> Recalls Early History of
> Truckee Meadows District
>
> Records back to 1874 Are Used in Action Argued Before
> Public Service Commission to Fix Water Rate;
> Legal Points Create Interest
>
> Turning back the pages of Truckee Meadows history and development for sixty years many farmers of the district have been digging up old deeds and contracts during the past few weeks to support their claims for free water service from two of the old ditches, that skirt the hills on the west side of the valley, carrying water from the Truckee river to nearly one hundred water-users.
>
> Actions before the Nevada public service commission, instituted on behalf of a large number of the farmers by Wayne T. Wilson, to have Last Chance ditch and the Lake ditch declared public utilities and the water service charges regulated by the commission, have brought out the historical discussions and also several technical legal points that are being given more than passing attention by attorneys.
>
> The Last Chance action was started several months ago while the action on the Lake ditch, similar in character, was started this week.
>
> The principal questions are involved:
> First: Whether or not the Nevada public service commission, which is not a judicial body, can ignore deeds and contracts held by many of the land-owners in the valley calling for free water from the ditches, and require them to pay for the water at a uniform rate.
> Second: Whether or not the Nevada public service com-

Eagles' Nest, Reno c. 1900 (west of corner of McCarran Blvd. and Plumb Lane today)

mission can declare the ditches public utilities, establish the values thereof, and regulate the rates to return a fair profit to the owners together with operating expenses.

Early in January the commission, which then consisted of J.F. Shaughnessy, H.R. Martin and George W. Malone, issued an order declaring that the Last Chance ditch was a public utility. At the same time Chairman Shaughnessy asserted that the commission would ignore free water deeds and early-day contracts calling for water at low and varying rates and establish a uniform rate for the seventy-five water-users supplied by the ditch.... Wilson represents about forty water-users from the Last Chance ditch, who have been paying as high as $7.50 per inch for their water, while W.M. Kearney represents several of the water-users who have old deeds or contracts, executed in their favor by the original owners of the ditch, providing that they shall have free water for all time.

Land owners now claiming free water service in the Last Chance ditch include:

Chrissie [sic] Caughlin 150 inches, L.W. Berrum 110 inches, Reno Golf Club 180 inches, Martha W. Landis 70 inches and United Nevada Bank 220 inches....

Both ditches are now owned by the United Nevada Bank and are being operated by Leo F. Schmitt, bank receiver, who takes the position that the free water service should be discontinued and that a uniform rate of $3.70 per inch established for all water-users on the Last Chance ditch....

The Last Chance ditch was built in 1874 by George W. Andrews, Enoch Morrill and Winslow P. Nay. Andrews owned ranch property west of Reno in the vicinity of the Old Mayberry ranch and built the first eight miles of the ditch taking water out of the Truckee river. Morrill extended the ditch to a point south and west of Moana Springs and nay extended it nearly to the Holcomb home ranch, making the entire ditch about seventeen miles long. The ditch has a capacity of 2500 inches but in the Talbot decree of 1915 it was allotted 1512 inches out of the Truckee river as representing the right of the various water-users being served by it....

A considerable part of the land supplied by the ditch has changed hands many times and the records introduced at the hearing disclosed the names of John Sparks, one-time governor of Nevada, Grove Holcomb, L. W. Berrum, James Mayberry, Barney Clow, M.L. Yager, Joseph Frey, W.R. Thompson, D.C. Wheeler, Chrissie Caughlin, J.W. Shaver, Peter Hanson, Ben Capurro, John Capurro and many others.

At the outset the ditch owners shared equally in the upkeep of the ditch but unlike many of the other ditch owners in this valley they did not organize a company and sell stock. The same is true of the Lake ditch.

Gradually the original owners disposed of their interests until finally the Holcomb estate acquired ownership of the entire ditch and the United Nevada Bank took it over when it took over the assets of the Realization Company. One of the last transactions made by the Holcomb estate involving the ditch was in 1929 when it purchased for $6000 175 inches of free water the ditch holdings of L.W. Berrum, which constituted about one-fifth of the ditch. Ownership of the ditch in itself carries no water rights....

One of the interesting phases of the proceedings on both ditches brought out at the hearings came when it was revealed that the Federal Land Bank holds mortgages on some of the ranches receiving free water service and in making the loan appraisements of the property took into consideration the value of the free water service.

In this connection it was pointed out that any action taken by the public service commission would probably be appealed to the state supreme court as a constitutional question is involved. The question is similar in principle to the gold clause question now before the United States supreme court, it was stated by attorneys, in that a contractual obligation is the focal point of the entire controversy.[3]

Irrigation Ditch
Not Utility is
Charge Made in Suit

Attacking the decision of the Nevada public service commission, which declared the Last Chance and Lake ditches to be common carriers and public utilities, Mrs. Crissie Caughlin filed a suit against the commission and Leo Schmitt, receiver of the United Nevada Bank. The bank is the owner of the Last Chance ditch, in which Mrs. Caughlin has a water right of 150 inches of water....

The suit denies that the ditch is a public utility or common carrier and declares that the public service commission's decision impairs the contract with the ditch owner, and denies the plaintiff her property.

The public service commission decided on April 15 that the Last Chance and Lake ditches are public utilities, and in the case of the Last Chance ditch, a charge of $2.50 an inch to all users was set. This rate was based on a valuation of $20,000 placed on the ditch by the commission, while Mrs. Caughlin's complaint sets the ditch value at $50,000.

A second suit against the Nevada public service commission over its decision regarding the Last Chance irrigation ditch was filed in the district court late yesterday afternoon. The plaintiffs are Ernest and B. Capurro, doing business as B. Capurro & Son, V. Piretto, D. Buscaglia and A. Schiappacasse....

There is some difficulty in following the course of the lawsuit, since it was first reported that Grandma Crissie and others filed the lawsuit against the Nevada Public Service Commission. The next article says that the Last Chance Ditch Company filed suit against Crissie

Last Chance Ditch Action
Draws to End
Final Arguments Set
For Friday by Court

Final arguments will be presented by attorneys next Friday in the district court here in the suit of the Last Chance Ditch Company against Mrs. Crissie Caughlan [sic], it was announced yesterday, when a two-day hearing in the suit ended before Judge William McKnight.

The ditch company, which owns the Last Chance Ditch... is suing Mrs. Caughlan in an attempt to terminate a water right agreement that has been in force for almost 60 years.

The Last Chance ditch was started in 1874 by the late George Andrews to supply water to his ranch west of Reno on the old Verdi road. Other farmers assisted in lengthening the ditch to their properties, and they were given interests in the canal until Andrews owned a nine-sixteenths interest in the property, it is claimed.

When Andrews later sold his interest in the ditch to James Mayberry, an agreement was made whereby it is claimed Andrews and his heirs could use 150 inches of water flowing in the ditch free of charge. The contract has been observed up to the present time, it is contended, and the Last Chance Ditch Company, which purchased the canal about two years ago is attempting to have it nullified.

Mrs. Caughlan is being sued as Andrews's heir.

Free Water Deeds Upheld by Court
[January 27, 1938, newspaper unknown]
Holders of deeds entitling them to the free transportation of irrigation water in the Last Chance ditch are not subject to the jurisdiction of the Nevada public service commission, which has designated the ditch as a public utility, Judge B. F. Curler held in a decision rendered yesterday in a suit filed against the commission by Mrs. Crissie Caughlin.

The ditch, now owned by the Last Chance Ditch Company, carries water to about forty-five Truckee Meadows ranchers, several of whom hold free water carrying deeds or contracts.

The ditch was located and constructed in 1874 by George W. Andrews, father of Mrs. Caughlin. Andrews, W.P. Nay, and Enoch Merrill acquired a right to 150 inches of water forever free from any assessments or charges and this right was written into deeds that were later sold or transferred with the land.

Last year the public service commission declared the Last Chance Ditch and the Lake ditches public utilities and fixed carrying charges based on valuations fixed for the two ditches.

Judge Clark Guild held several months ago that holders of deeds or contracts entitling them to water free of the ditch charges in the Lake ditch could not be forced to pay for them.

Holders of free water deeds in the Last Chance ditch, in addition to Mrs. Caughlin are V. Piretto, Capurro Brothers, D. Buscaglia, A. Schiappacasse, A. Baroli and the Frey ranch.

W.M. Kearney represented Mrs. Caughlin in the court action.

Recently the Last Chance Ditch Company petitioned the public service commission to increase the water carrying charge to $5.10 per inch from $2.50 per inch. A hearing will probably be held on the petition after February 1.

Although Crissie's water rights were upheld in the 1930s, the battle returned in 1949, as I found in a few of her letters.

Thursday, August 18, 1949

Dear Betsy,
 I know you are as anxious as I am to know how things are going. I'm just holding my breath to see what happens before the sun goes down tonight. Kearney [attorney W.M Kearney, who was Grandma Crissie's lawyer] has eight pages and everything set so I can have my heirs enjoy my perpetual water rights, if I get it…. I think the fellows have quit until the papers are signed, and we are both Scotch; for how long, I don't know. My water is still flowing….

Tuesday, August 24

Dear Betsy
 I don't have to hold my breath any longer. I have to breathe long and deep. I'm up against a condemnation suit, but it will be settled one way or t'other. I will or I won't have my perpetual flow of free water. Woodburn, Thatcher & Thompson served the papers on me and the Land Bank. I went down yesterday and saw Mr. Tregaro. He is going to Berkeley today, and he would explain to them. He said the bank would stand pat with me—their attorneys will—if they have had any cases like this. Will give my attorney their opinion. Well, anyway, Bill Kearney told me not to worry, and I haven't lost any sleep so far….

Tuesday, August 30

Dear Betsy,
 …my water case came up yesterday. Wes and Sy went, but Kearney thought I better stay home, which I did and cleaned Bill's room…. Bill [Kearney] is surely making it tough on the Power Company. If he wins that suit, it will sure add another red feather in his cap and he is doing his darndest.
 Wes looks fine…. Now he is eligible for a G.I. Loan and wants to buy the Jap Flat. I told him he was crazy. He did not know a thing about the business. He said he would learn and Bill would help him. People think there is nothing to learn about ranching, but just look pretty and go fishing or play with the dog or cat….

September 23, 1949

Dear Betsy,

You will say Mother is wrong somehow; the clipping might help to explain. I haven't heard anything, only what is in the papers. Sometimes I think if I had gone to the high officials and told them I wanted a transfer of my water and not gone to Kearney, it might have been better, and I would have gotten the perpetual right transferred....

Bill Kearney just called and wanted to know if I was willing to have this statement transferred (the water) to another channel. By the laws of the new company, they are not allowed to grant free water, but this perpetual right holds good to be transferred to another channel, which I agreed to. They are in a hurry to proceed. If it goes to court, it has to be decided by the Supreme Court, and that they don't want to be on the records. They were in his office this morning to find out if I would agree to the transfer. It must be the perpetual right holds good or they would not take the time or bother, but would fight to the finish. I told Bill to tell them to make it a perpetual right as long as the Caughlin family were in existence, and we shouldn't worry about anyone else....

Love, Mother[4]

Thus ended the court battle in which Crissie preserved the perpetual water rights for the Caughlin Ranch. It lasted from 1913 to 1949.

CHAPTER ELEVEN
Caughlin Ranch Development

As a child, I hiked all over Crissie's ranch. When I look at it now, Stonegate development is where the rocky pasture was and is probably where photos of the haystacks were taken. From today's River Run development and going east nearly to Ferris Street was called the Lower Ranch. On the same side of the street as the ranch house, what is now Mayberry Meadows development was the entrance to the Caughlin Ranch. Patches of the old Verdi Road are still visible nearby. The dead tree in the pasture behind the house was once a big, beautiful cottonwood, and nearby was Crissie's apple orchard. She showed me where her father had planted a grapevine from New Hampshire.

The original ranch house that George built sat near the corner of Plumb Laneand McCarran Boulevard. It was later moved to the present location, added onto in 1948, and became the bunkhouse. Later, the northeast corner of Plumb and McCarran was called Jap Flat, where several Japanese families rented small plots for growing vegetables. My mother Syrene and her second husband came to live near there in 1953. Crissie loved having Syrene back on the ranch, so she gave them the land on Plumb Lane. While their house was being built, Crissie came to visit, and my mother would put a chair outside so Crissie could sit and view her ranch from their home on the hill.

Crissie's property eventually reached from the Truckee River to what is now Skyline Boulevard. She sold only a few pieces of land during her lifetime. Horseman's Park went to the City of Reno, because she loved horses so much. She to the Carmelite nuns, where they built their monastery. She also sold one piece of land off of Knight Road to Chick Callahan, who milked cows for her, because he begged to buy the land when he married. She also sold land to Judge John Belton and his wife Marion, for a house and horses.

Her property extended to the southwest beyond Eagle's Nest, obviously named for a nest of eagles that lived there. Beyond that was Snow Lake, a small lake where my mother once rode her horse when she was a girl. At one time, Crissie told me she owned 6, 000 acres.

The ranch Crissie left to her children was 3,100 acres and spanned 3½ miles deep and 3 miles across at the widest point. Three major irrigation ditches crossed the land – the Lake Ditch, Steamboat Ditch and Last Chance Ditch.

The ranch house, originally a home that was moved from Virginia City in 1900 by railroad and wagon to its present site, is still standing on Mayberry Drive.

In her will, Crissie left the ranch in joint ownership to her three children—William Caughlin, Syrene Seagrave, and Elizabeth Donnelly. In order to pay the inheritance taxes on Crissie's estate, two sections of land near Skyline Boulevard were sold.

Bill Jr. continued to live at the ranch until his death in 1983, although he was a ward of the court due to his World War I injuries.

Ranch before development

WILLIAM CAUGHLIN

William H(ughes) "Bill" Caughlin, a member of the pioneer Nevada family that had owned the Caughlin Ranch since 1874, died Wednesday in a Reno care center. He was 88.

The Reno native was born Nov. 25, 1895, to William Henry and Crissie Andrews Caughlin. His grandfather, George Washington Andrews, built the Steamboat Ditch by pick and shovel, according to his family. Caughlin's father was Washoe County sheriff 1892-1896.

Caughlin had been a rancher.

A graveside funeral and burial with full military honors is scheduled....[2]

DEVELOPING THE RANCH

I met Don Lonie on May 1, 1980 in Honolulu at the home of my dear friend, Alyce Craft. At the time, I had been a widow for two years, and Don's wife had passed away a few months earlier. Don had been in Hawaii for about 10 years. He had developed three condominium projects on Maui and also bought many individual condos on Maui and Oahu.

My friend Alyce told him of my family's ranch in Reno, owned by my mother, Syrene Caughlin Seagrave, my Aunt Betsy Caughlin Donnelly, and Uncle William Caughlin in "undivided thirds." They were all in their eighties and were being told by their attorneys that the land should be sold, because much of it would be lost to taxes as soon as any one of them died.

Ranch before development

Don Lonie called me a few weeks after my return. He was in town and was eager to see the ranch. Don had already met my mother in Hawaii, so I introduced him to Aunt Betsy and Uncle Bill. Then I took my Jeep and drove him all over the ranch. He later said he lost his heart twice that day—once when he saw me and a second time when he saw the untouched ranch land. It was the most spectacular land he had ever seen.

Don talked to our attorney, Russ MacDonald, who had been a dear friend of the family for many years. Russ's mother and Crissie were dear friends, and Aunt Betsy babysat with Russ when he was a youngster. Russ was delighted that Don wanted to option the whole ranch, nearly 3,000 acres. Don hired Bill Kimmel, Reno's number one land surveyor and also a family friend; his mom and aunt were friends of my mother and aunt.

Don spent the next two years having the property surveyed. He was a visionary, and during that time his dream for the ranch property took shape. He created a master plan and had a topical map of the entire ranch made based on that plan. Alan Means was the engineer, and Sam Jaksick was the financial backer.

Don's dream was to retain the feeling of wide-open spaces, partly with walking paths and jogging trails. He envisioned a fitness center, a school, and a shopping center. Small apartments were planned along the Truckee River. It was very important to Don that the last link of McCarran Boulevard should wind through the ranch in such a way that it would not destroy or divide the natural beauty of the land. Alum Creek was to have family homes; next came the town houses; then the gated community featuring large custom homes; and finally, near the top of the ridge would be the 10 and 40-acre lots.

Ranch before development

There were two sections of property on the top ridge that were covered with pines. It took three years, but Don traded that beautiful forested land to the BLM so that no one could ever build on it.

Once the master plan was finished, a large community gathering was held. After the plan was shown and everyone understood how carefully the 3,000 acres would be developed, there were very few objections.

Don expected the development to take 20 years to build out, but it was finished in just 10 years. The development won awards for the design, and so many of those who see the ranch or who live on the property say it is the finest development ever built in Reno.

In early promotional material, Don said:

Don Lonie, Caughlin Ranch, Reno 1982

Just 3½ minutes from downtown Reno lies the 3,100 acre Caughlin Ranch, the most spectacular piece of undeveloped urban property in all of Nevada. The Caughlin family has held this property together in one magnificent parcel while the city of Reno has grown around and past it.

Nearly every point of the Caughlin Ranch offers a breathtaking view of Reno and the surrounding area. Most sites on the ranch provide a 360-degree panorama of snow-capped mountains, the bustling metropolitan valley, and peaceful tree-carpeted forests. Even the air is beautiful.

I have the highest pleasure in being involved with this outstanding property, as it develops to become one of Reno's finest neighborhoods.

The Caughlin Ranch sits astride one of the nation's rare geo-thermal areas, providing free sources of home heating and water heating by simply drilling a well.

I invite your interest.

Cordially,
D. Donald Lonie, Jr.

Don and I were married May 29, 1984. He died on May 12, 1997, after an amazing life. A graduate from the University of Oregon School of Journalism, he was a pioneer in TV broadcasting, serving as the promotion and sales manager for the first commercial UHF station in the world in 1962. He helped negotiate programming agreements for the Pacific Northwest, and in that role, he hosted TV stars such as Arlene Francis, Jack Parr, Sid Caesar, and Imogene Cocoa.

He went on to own his own public relations firm, co-founded the Oregon Museum of Science and Industry, and served on numerous civic groups. He served on the Board of Governors for the Montreux Golf Course and the Board of Trustees of Sierra Nevada College. Don lived long enough to see so much of his dream realized for the Caughlin Ranch development. Although he is gone, his vision for our family's ranch is his legacy to all of us.

TWO PARKS

On Nov. 5, 1993, Betsy Caughlin Donnelly donated 30 acres of land adjacent to the Caughlin Ranch house at the corner of Mayberry Drive and McCarran Boulevard to Washoe County as a park named in her honor. The County Commissioners accepted the land, including water rights. Betsy was born in one of the bedrooms of the old ranch house and graduated from Reno High School in 1921. She lived with her husband Roger Donnelly in San Francisco for 25 years, and returned to Reno when he retired in the 1960s.

In addition, the Crissie Caughlin Park is located near the Truckee River. The location of the park named for her would please Crissie, because she never wanted to see houses built right up to the edge of the river.

RESTORATION OF THE RANCH HOUSE

The ranch house had spent many years empty or rented and therefore fell into disrepair. Crissie lived in the bunkhouse during the winters, because the ranch house was too cold. Betsy retained the ranch house and some of the adjacent property when the Caughlin Ranch development began. She paid my son Richard Scharbach, an engineer, to save the beautiful old ranch house.

RANCH HOUSE RESTORATION BY RICHARD SCHARBACH

In early 1993, the old ranch house had been empty for almost five years and was looking as peaked as any abandoned 93-year-old house would. The porch was rotting and damaged by the overgrowth of grapevines, originally from New Hampshire. The area near the back door area was damaged by water leaks from the bathroom above on the second floor, which was a poorly crafted room and suffered years of abuse from renters. The whole interior of the ranch house was pretty beat up. The 50-year-old electrical wiring system was an extreme fire hazard. The plumbing was choked with mineral buildup. The old roofs had been repaired, but replacements were nailed on top of the old one, each time adding to the overall weight of the roof.

In the spring of 1993, my Great Aunt Betsy Donnelly and I decided to collaborate our efforts and bring the great old house, where she was born in 1902, back to it's former glory. I committed my time and energy (not to mention my blood, sweat, and tears) to the project, and Betsy agreed to fund it. While dismantling the house, I engaged the services of my old college architectural professor, Brad Van Woert, who now practices in Reno, to help me modify the outdated Victorian floor plan to a more practical and modern version designed to help the flow of foot traffic.

The demolition phase took over a year and filled 20, 20-yard dumpsters full of old flooring, lath and plaster, and seven layers of shingles and composition roofing material, along with the entire porch and kitchen. Before the actual demolition began came the task of removing all of the leftover furniture and personal items that had survived the years. Under one of the beds in the upstairs southwest bedroom, I found newspapers from the turn of the century and a cloth map of the United States, circa 1851. There was no such a thing as a carpet pad in those days, so these common, everyday items were used to cushion the feet. Stremmel Galleries in Reno sent the map back to a special restoration house in Ohio to preserve it and keep it from further decomposition.

I've wondered whether my Great Great Grandfather George Andrews or a member of the Hughes family first used the map when they came to Nevada in the 1850s. The age of the map reflected the era and denoted Canada as "British Holdings." During the lath and plaster removal phase, I discovered inside the kitchen wall a handful of perfectly preserved square nails. They looked as though they came fresh from a Reno general store, circa 1900, when the house was said to have been brought down from Virginia City on the Virginia & Truckee Railroad and rebuilt on the spot where it stands today. Also, in that wall I found a handful of a child's homemade marbles. When I showed them to Betsy, she didn't know to whom the marbles belonged, but that made sense, because she was born in the house after that wall was finished. Grandma Crissie told my mother the marbles belonged to Rowland. The exterior of the house is made of redwood shiplap siding with dimensions straight out of the 19th century. To replace the areas on the west and south sides of the house, where the weathering was most severe, required a special milling ordered through Steve Mikkelson, a brother of an old friend of mine, at Piedmont Lumber Co., in Oakland, California. All of the exterior window and door trim moldings also had to be ordered through Piedmont Lumber. My friend and master woodcrafter and antique restorer, Kris Mikkelson, recreated the trim scheme, which consisted of nine separate moldings. He was able to make them to match the window and door trims that were still intact on the north and east sides of the house.

The old porch was eight feet wide, whereas the new one is now ten feet wide. That required incorporating the old columns and combining them with newer, cast columns to support the larger porch. The old porch started at the kitchen and wrapped around the house, where it stopped at the extension line of the west side of the house. That west wall of the porch was originally closed in with two sets of metal-framed windows to block the prevailing west winds. That area was also screened to keep the flies out—typical of a working cattle ranch on hot summer days. For the new porch, I eliminated the windows and continued around the northwest corner of the house to a wooden stairway that leads to the west side of the house.

A new, sweeping, brick front stair makes the front entrance a little grander than the old wooden stairway. The original front door and cabinetry exterior alcove was stripped of all the many layers of old paint to bring alive the Victorian style that once graced that area. A Victorian patterned etched glass was added, which ended up being fancier than the original, as is the one in the front stairs. We recreated the ceiling of the porch with a wainscoting wood and painted it sky blue. Legend has it that blue is supposed to keep the flies off, but I always preferred Grandmother Syrene's reason for the color; "one would always have a blue sky, even on a gray rainy day".

The old kitchen was a two-sectioned room with the pantry area separated by a wall from the main room. The original kitchen had a sink and a wood-burning stove. In later years, an electric stove plus a breakfast nook with a small table and chairs was added. The new kitchen combined the two areas to make a single, open, and flowing kitchen with an island in the middle. Cabinets from Pennsylvania adorn the majority of the walls. Flooring of travertine marble and counters of Canadian green granite with an OG edge finished the kitchen remodel.

With demolition complete, the whole interior of the house was exposed down to the original two-by-six studs. These rough-hewn, structural members were the real things; two inches by six inches, not like "modern" dimensions that are 1 1/2" by 5 1/2". Upon inspection, the split granite foundation, manufactured of large granite boulders from the surrounding meadows, and the main structure of the house were not only plumb and square, but in remarkable shape considering their age. The limestone based mortar that held together the granite and the river rock foundation under the kitchen all those years had to be sandblasted out. Cementicious mortar replaced it to restore the strength and integrity of the foundation.

The house was now ready for the new electrical and plumbing plans, which included a sound system and alarm system throughout—modern additions. The interior wood trim on the windows and doors was destroyed in the demolition phase. The old double-hung windows, with weights and pulleys, were replaced with double pane Architectural Series Pella windows that were sized to slide up against the preserved exterior trim. That made the outside view of the house look entirely Victorian. Piedmont Lumber Co. milled not only the exterior siding and trim, but also many board feet of interior window and door trim. A one-piece baseboard trim was created from the original four smaller molding combination "stacked" baseboard. Before that baseboard was installed, the two main hallways in the house along with the dining room had to be fitted with red oak hardwood flooring to match the flooring in the "parlor" area of the house.

The basement, which is located under the kitchen, had an old "Dorothy and Toto" type storm door that allowed workers and family members an outside access for storing garden produce. However, the door and incorporated stairway were in very bad shape, so we filled the opening with a stand-up safe and backfilled behind it with concrete and earth. This eliminated an unsecured entrance into the house and, at the same time, incorporated an in-house safety deposit box of grand proportions.

In the original scheme of the house, there was no fireplace. There were three chimneys, which were used with the kitchen stove and smaller woodburning stoves. Above each of the interior doors were transoms that could be opened and closed according to that particular room's need for heat. The transoms and all interior doors were meticulously sanded, repainted, and refitted with modern brass to keep the Victorian flavor of the house intact. The kitchen chimney was torn down during the demolition phase, because it didn't fit with a modern kitchen. The remaining two chimneys were left intact and exposed in each of the rooms. This keeps open an emergency venue for woodburning stoves in the event of a future fossil fuel crisis. We wanted to install a fireplace, but that was not allowed due to Washoe County Health Standards. Both stories of the house were outfitted with propane burning furnaces to keep the newly insulated house warm in the coldest of winters.

The original house had an open attic large enough for a tennis court, but it was not used except for access to the roof through a cap in the top of the pyramid shaped roof. We designed a small storage room for this area, with a dormer window facing south for a unique, elevated view of the Betsy Caughlin Donnelly Park. We built in bookcases with glass doors and lighting to display treasures. A four-by-four-foot hinged skylight was built into the top of the upper roof to allow natural sunlight in and summer heat out. The installation of that skylight was a "three try" comedy of errors. On the first try, the skylight was set on top of the house with a crane. It was a windy day, and the main carpenter (me) forgot to nail it temporarily in place. A big gust of wind came through the dormer window opening and blew the skylight off the top of the house, in a "Pop goes the Weasel" kind of scenario, to it's final resting place on the front lawn. The amazed looks I got from passers-by as I shop-vacuumed the pile of broken safety glass off the lawn was funny. The second skylight was craned into place a month later and immediately nailed into place. That night it rained. The next day was cold enough to freeze the puddle that had formed on the glass into an ice rink, and the Canadian geese took advantage of it by landing on it and skating, too. Subsequently, the glass broke for a second time, adding insult to injury. The third time was charmed and the skylight was installed.

The staircase to the attic area was designed as a built-in, hardwood spiral staircase and features the salvaged spindles from the original open staircase between the first and second floors. The upstairs and downstairs hallways were six feet wide, but the old staircase took up half of that width on both floors. By making the staircase a little wider and moving it to the east hallway wall, we sacrificed a little space in each of the rooms, but reopened the two hallways to their six-foot-wide glory. The two den/study rooms on the first floor—originally the parlors—are now smaller, but underneath the staircase on the first floor, we add a half-bath. The old rooms used for butter churning and reading, on the southwest corner of the first floor, were changed into a modern laundry room and a TV room, respectively. Thus, the downstairs floor plan was changed very little in the restoration process.

In order to keep the outside of the house true to it's original design and appearance, the window locations where kept the same. This meant that almost every wall had a low/high window in the middle of the wall, making the rooms difficult to furnish. A sun deck was added to the south end of the house on the second floor over the kitchen. The architect and I designed a unique double set of joists; one has a slight slope to hold the rubberized roof that drains rain water out to scuppers and downspouts; and the second has a level set of joists that supports the sun deck above the rubberized roof. A window was changed into a door to the sun deck, which is now off of the expanded master bedroom.

Another friend, Van Frank, came out from Pennsylvania to do the red composition roof. The four other outbuildings adjacent to the house were subsequently topped with the same red comp roofing material to give the place a red roof, white exterior paint, and blue porch ceiling—an all American look.

The bunkhouse, located behind the ranch house, was originally used as sleeping quarters for the ranch hands. At the time the small, two-room building was moved down the hill and extra rooms were added on to make it more habitable. The old shack behind the bunkhouse that housed chickens blew halfway over in the winter of 1982-1983. It was demolished, then rebuilt that summer as a storage and game shack.

The old tin garage with its earthen floors was converted into a modern, three-car garage with concrete slab floors and electric door openers during the year following the restoration of the ranch house. The old well was repaired with river rock. The new concrete cap made with metal ties supports a new and historically correct version of a pyramid roof and cross support pulley system for a water bucket. However, the well water now comes from the irrigated field water, and silt has filled in the bottom of the well so that it cannot accommodate a water bucket. The original driveway ran along the east side of the ranch house between the well and the house, but it was moved east along the tree line to keep big delivery trucks from hitting the well.

In 1997, the City of Reno's Historical Resources Commission bestowed upon me the "Historic Preservation Award for a Residential Structure." The plaque states, "In recognition of your outstanding efforts on behalf of Historic Preservation and Commitment to Maintenance and Preservation of The Caughlin Ranch House."

CHAPTER TWELVE
Crissie's Final Goodbye

CRISSIE'S FINAL YEARS were filled with happiness. The Grandma Crissie I remember was always happy. She had a sunny disposition and a warm heart, always generous with her home and food. She loved people and made time for friends and family. Men loved her intelligence and incredible sense of humor. She seemed to have inherited her father George's charm and the Hughes family's love of fun. Every afternoon, Crissie would dress up and go to the grocery store to talk to the butcher and clerks and to visit with friends and acquaintances. She had a great zest for life and was active in clubs—the Garden Gate Club, the Homemakers, and Eastern Star. In her steady correspondence with her daughters in the Bay Area, she mentioned her social outings.

Monday a.m.

>I have to draw this to a close as I am going to a Garden Gate Club.
>With love from Mother

December 20, 1944

Dear Betsy,
.... I would like to go to [Eastern] Star tonight. The two chapters are having installation. It is like a dress parade—everybody all dolled up and a good program.

Thursday, October 12, 1945

My Dear Betsy,
.... Mrs. John Davidson, who lives now on Plumb Lane, is having a flower show Monday. I'm going to take that bunch of potted geraniums you fixed. They are all full of bloom. I have them here on the porch and they are so pretty....

Asa Weston Seagrave, Pilot, b. April 27, 1922, San Francisco, d. 1991, Reno, Nv

Betsy Caughlin at her park dedication

December 2, 1945

My Dear Betsy,

.... Tomorrow my Garden Gate [club] meets. We will have a Christmas party on the 11th. Our Homemakers meet for another Christmas party.

Grandma Crissie enjoyed her freedom and independence, and she spent any leisure time reading and going to movies.

Thursday, March 29, 1945

My Dear Betsy,

I ran in to see Minerva [Pierce, first president of the Latimer Club] yesterday and she has been down in bed again. She is up and sitting around playing Canasta to keep Ed from going nuts. Gee, I'm glad I don't have to entertain a man. I can rest or work or <u>go</u> and no comment.

March 23, 1946

My Dear Betsy,

I did not like [the movie] "Blue Skies" as well as "Holiday in Mexico." The scenery was beautiful; their costumes were very good. Jane Powee, a new artist, was cute and a good singer. The music was extra and everything about the show was good.

Love, Mother

Wednesday, April 2, 1947

My Dear Betsy,

I've got a few moments to spend with you. Today is Home Makers Day and demonstrations on rug making, for those who don't how....

Wish I could have seen "The Student Prince." Those things never come to Reno. I have the book, *The Three Musketeers*. "The Song of Norway" is very highly advertised. I have a copy, one of the first ones, of *Big Bonanza*, but I keep it in my back closet. I've lost so many books by just leaving them out. I can't remember about *Alice in Wonderland*, if I gave it to some youngster....

I got the suit altered you gave me and it is at the cleaners. Min gave me that brown suit with the pin stripe, too small for her and very good on me with very little alteration. [Waste not, want not was one of my grandmother's favorite sayings.]

April 16, 1947

My Dear Betsy,

If you can get *Collier's* [magazine] issue of April 19, there is an article and picture of Mrs. John Mackay, or Mrs. Bonanza, as she was called... but it does not tell of her educating Emma Wixom I can see by this article how Emma got the notice she received in Europe through Mrs. Mackay, although she did sing well and made several tours. But a girl has to have someone to promote those tours....

We had a nice trip last Sunday. Al took the Cadillac, Min, Sy, and myself and went to the lake. We went by Truckee and around to Tallac. We had a nice time and came home by Carson....

Christine Andrews Caughlin, Richard Edward Scharbach. Christmas, 1953. Her third great grandchild

May 26, 1949

.... By the way, if "Mr. Belvedere Goes to College" with Shirley Temple comes, which it will, it was filmed in Reno, and I think you will like it.

February 3, 1950

Dear Betsy,

.... I did have a good time at the pioneer party. Saw Mrs. Keel. She said they are still talking about it. None of them are as old as I am and not Nevada born. They are a Mormon group. I lived here when Nevada was a territory. No, not me, but my parents, located in 1864 in Washoe....

Love, Mother

Grandma Crissie also loved the ranch and continued to oversee the work. Now, with the Depression and war years behind her, she was able to leave the ranch more often. She learned to drive a car by trial and error one day after a picnic. She went with her daughters, Syrene and Betsy, for a picnic at Bowers Mansion. When it came time to go home, the girls wanted to go with friends by way of Virginia City. They showed Crissie how to operate the car, and with no practice or experience, she drove the car home. When she was 70 years old, she took her Buick with its rumble seat and drove all the way to Berkeley by herself to visit my mother Syrene.

She adored her two grandchildren, my brother Weston and me, and her great grandchildren. When Weston's son Robert (nicknamed Button) was teething, Crissie used one of her home remedies and gave him a "sugar tit," which was a bit of bourbon and a sugar cube in a cloth. Crissie also had great pa-

Crissie at Shiela's wedding. Alyce. Dr. Robert Scharbach, D.D.S.; new wife Shiela; Marian Seagrave, fraternal grandmother; Seated, Crissie Caughlin, maternal grandmother.

Crissie Caughlin and family at Stacie's christening, 1950. Bob and Shiela Scharbach, baby Stacie Christine, Gale King, god-mother, Weston Seagrave god-father. St. Marks, Berkeley, California

tience with children and was always ready to join in a game of make-believe. One day

Button came to her and said, "Grandma, come outside and shoot the bird." Crissie got up from the dinner table, went outside with Button, and pretended to shoot the bird.

When my daughter Stacie was 10 months old and lying on a blanket outdoors, Crissie took a stick and stirred the anthills, which entertained Stacie for an hour. She was enchanted. When my brother and I were children, Grandma Crissie would get out the pots and pans, or she would have a flat stick with wax paper on it to stick into the honeycombs for a sweet treat.

My mother gave a wonderful description of Crissie in one of her letters.

Friday, November 8, 1946

Dear Betsy and Rog,

.... I simply refuse to go to any Garden Gate or Homemakers clubs. I'll drive her there and call for her, but nothing doing otherwise. She's tried every way—"just run in for a minute." But I won't budge.... I try not to let mother do any dishes and make her sit and read or sleep after dinner. But she surely has the work laid out for you every a.m....

Yesterday she wore her new dress to the Century Club.... She looked awfully cute. I made her wear my aqua ear-

Crissies' daughters Betsy and Syrene

rings, which just matched the dress. She felt so conscious with them on, but when she came home, she was happy, as everyone told her how snappy she looked, and Mrs. Green said she could tell she had been down to California to see her girls. I noticed she didn't take the earrings off until time to go to bed.

Be seeing you both,
Love Sy

Dedication of the park, Nov. 10, '93

Friday, January 10, 1947

Dear Betsy,

This is a quickie! I darn near phoned you yesterday a.m. to come on up. We have had a very sick little mother. Even I was a little frightened, but now with care, she'll be OK.... I finally got Dr. Lynn Guow out about 5 p.m., but she was a little better by then. He wrote a prescription for her, but I have a heck of a time getting her to take it. She is a good patient otherwise, sleeping most of the time. She had some cream of wheat last night… and a cup of tea…. She is very much better this p.m. but Dr. said she'd have to stay in bed a few days. Shiela has been a godsend—cooking, shopping, and washing dishes....

Love, Sy and Shiela

September 16, 1949

Dear Betsy,

I had a lot of fun last Saturday—went to Mrs. John Davidson's home party and Eilley Orrum tea. I wore the old brown silk dress and with the parasol. They all through I looked "cute" – next to the oldest dress there… mine was 1869 or 1870….

Love, Mother

Clara Crisles of Carson City and Crissie Caughlin of Reno at a tea held to raise funds for the Bowers' Mansion at the home of Mrs. John Davidson, Sept. 1944. Persia Bowers was a childhood friend of Crissie's

The last time I saw Grandma Crissie, she was staying in the bunkhouse. Bob and I had just returned from Hawaii, where he attended a dental convention for three weeks.

Crissie gave me her diamond engagement ring. Then she said, "Syrene, Betsy, and Shiela, hold my hands. I want to feel your energy going through my body. What would I do without my girls?"

My mother had to take Crissie to a nursing home for her final days. Mother was driving, and Crissie asked her to slow down as they were driving past the Ferris' peach orchards, which were located about where Raley's is now at the corner of Mayberry and Hunter Lake.

"Goodbye Ferris'. Goodbye Shiappacasses." Crissie was saying goodbye to all of her friends and neighbors. She knew she would not return to the ranch.

As she lay dying at the nursing home she said, "I'm ready to go now. My mother needs me." Crissie was Bettie's only surviving child, and she always felt responsible for her mother's care.

My Aunt Betsy was in tears and said, "Don't leave. We need you."

Crissie's final words were, "No, my mother needs me more."

Crissie died in 1955, just one month before her 89th birthday.

My favorite picture of Crissie. It shows her sparkling eyes, her good humor and love of life — with broom in hand.

LONG TIME RENO RESIDENT DIES

CHRISSIE CAUGHLIN
RITES ARE PENDING

Member of a pioneer Nevada family and a resident of the Reno vicinity for more than 80 years, Mrs. Chrissie (sic) Caughlin died today [August 3, 1955] at a local rest home at the age of 88.

Mrs. Caughlin, widow of William H. Caughlin, former rancher who served six years as sheriff of Washoe county, made her home on her ranch on Mayberry road, once the Verdi highway, until a short time ago when she entered a rest home.

BORN IN WASHOE

She was born in Washoe City, Sept. 6, 1866, the daughter of Mr. and Mrs. George W. Andrews, pioneer settlers of the state. After attending school in Washoe she came to Reno as a student at the Bishop Whitaker School for girls, and later attended University of Nevada normal school. She and Mr. Caughlin were married in 1895.

ACTIVE IN CLUBS

In addition to supervising the operation of her ranch Mrs. Caughlin was active in lodge and club circles. She was a member of Nevada chapter No. 13, Order of the Eastern Star, Garden Gate Club and the Home Makers.

Surviving are two daughters... Syrene... of Reno and Mrs. Roger (Betsy) Donnelly of San Francisco; a son, William H. Caughlin of Reno; and two grandchildren, Mrs. Shiela Scharbach of Berkeley and Weston Seagrave of the U.S. Air Force in Georgia. Also surviving are three great-grandchildren.[1]

Crissie's Descendents

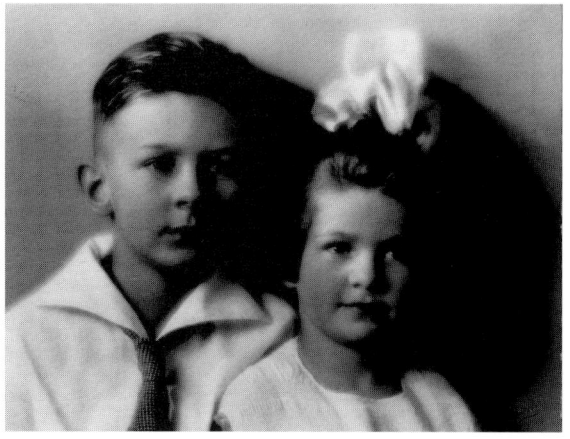
Weston and Shiela Seagrave, Christmas 1930

Shiela Seagrave, 1942

Shiela Lonie

Lt. Asa Weston Seagrave and Robert Weston Seagrave, b. July 30, 1945

Robert, Mille and Weston Seagrave, Texas, 1964

Syrene Seagrave and Syrene Scharbach. May Day, 1969

Richard Edward Scharbach, b. October 1, 1953, Berkeley, CA

Lee Ann Scharbach, b. December 10, 1993, Reno, NV

Syrene Francis (Scharbach), b. February 24, 1959, Berkeley, CA

Steven Tyler Francis, August 12, 1986, Walnut Creek, CA

John Hunter Francis, b. August1, 1988, Walnut Creek, CA

Grace Francis. b. 1995, Walnut Creek, CA

Stacie (Scharbach Williamson) Lee

Whitney Williamson, b. December 30, 1977

Robert Bruce Williamson, b. December 1, 1981, Berkeley, CA

Great Grandmother Crissie Caughlin and Stacie Scharbach

The Four Generations, Easter, May 14, 1978
Whitney Williamson, Shiela Scharbach, Syrene Seagrave, Stacie Williamson. Claremont C. C., Oakland, CA

APPENDIX

Crissie's Library

Crissie was born into a literate family and education was important to George and the Andrews family. George gave Crissie many books, and among them were reference books on ranching.

Beecher, Harriet, *Miss Beecher's Domestic Receipt-Book, Third Edition.* New York: Harper & Brothers, Publishers, 1860.
[This book belonged to Betsy H. Andrews, 1863, and a stamp said it was purchased from Mosse & Son, Books, Stationery, Periodicals, and Yankee Notions, No. 639 Kearny Street, Near Clay, San Francisco]

"Designed as a Supplement to her Treatise on Domestic Economy."
CONTENTS
Chapter I, On Selecting Food and Drinks with Reference to Health
Chapter II, Marketing – Care and Uses of Meats
Chapter III, Boiled Meats
Chapter IV, Roasted and Baked Meats
Chapter V, Fried and Broiled Meats
Chapter VI, Soups
Chapter VII, Fish
Chapter VIII, On the Preparation of Hashes, Gravies, and Sauces
Chapter IX, Vegetables
Chapter X, Ovens, Yeast, Bread, and Biscuit
Chapter XI, Breakfast and Tea Cakes
Chapter XII, Plain Puddings and Pies
Chapter XIII, Rich Puddings and Pies
Chapter XIV, Plain Cakes
Chapter, XV, Rich Cakes
Chapter XVI, Preserves and Jellies
Chapter XVII, Pickles
Chapter XVIII, Articles for Desserts and Evening Parties
Chapter XIX, Temperance Drinks
Chapter XX, Receipts for Food and Drinks for the Sick
Chapter XXI, On Making Butter and Cheese
Chapter XII, Articles and Conveniences for the Sick
Chapter XXIII, The Providing and Care of Family Stores
Chapter XXIV, Suggestions in Reference to providing a Successive Variety of Food
Chapter XXV, On Bread Making
Chapter XXVI, Directions for Dinner and Evening Parties

Chapter XXVII, On Setting Tables, and Preparing Various Articles of Food for the Table
Chapter XXVIII, On Systematic Family Arrangement, and Mode of Doing Work
Chapter XXIX, On a Proper Supply of Utensils and Conveniences for Housekeeping
Chapter XXX, Suggestions in Regard to Hired Services
Chapter XXXI, On the Style of Living and Expenses
Chapter XXXII, Words of Comfort for a Discouraged Housekeeper
Chapter XXIII, Friends Counsels for Domestics
Chapter XXXIV, Miscellaneous Advice, and Supplementary Receipts

From Chapter XXVIII

On Systematic Family Arrangement, and Mode of Doing Work.

Nothing secures ease and success in housekeeping so efficiently as *system* in arranging work. In order to aid those who are novices in these matters, the following outlines are furnished by an accomplished housekeeper. They are the details of family work, in a family of ten persons, where a cook, chambermaid, and boy, are all the domestics employed, and where the style of living is plain, but every way comfortable. The mistress of this family arranges the work for each domestic, and writes it on a large card, which is suspended in the kitchen for guidance and reference....

Directions for the Cook

Sunday – Rise as early as on other days. No work is to be done that can be properly avoided.

Monday – Rise early in hot weather, to have the cool of the day for work. Try to have everything done in the best manner. See that the clothesline is brought in at night, and the clothespins counted and put in the bag. Put the tubs, barrel, and pails used, on the cellar bottom.

Inquire every night, before going to bed, respecting breakfast, so as to make preparation beforehand.

Tuesday – Clean the kitchen and sink-room. Bake, and fold the clothes to iron the next day.

Wednesday – Rise early in warm weather, so as to iron in the cool of the day.

Thursday – Fold off the clothes. No other special work.

Friday – Clean all the closets, the kitchen windows, the cellar stairs, and the privies. Try up all the grease, and put it away for use.

Saturday – Bake, and prepare a dinner for Sunday.

Every day but Monday, wipe the shelves in the pantry and kitchen closet.

Be careful to have clean dishtowels, and never use them for other purposes.

Keep a good supply of holders, both for cooking and ironing, and keep them hung up when not in use.

Keep your boiler for dishwater covered.

Sweep and dust the kitchen every day.
Never throw dirt, bones, or paper around the doors or yard.
Never give or lend what belongs to the family without leave.
Try to keep everything neat, clean, and in order.
Have a time for everything, a place for everything, and everything in its place.
The hour for going to bed is ten o'clock. Those who work hard should go to bed early, or else health and eyesight will fail. [p. 247-248]

From Chapter XXXII

Words of Comfort for a Discouraged Housekeeper

There is no doubt of the fact, that American housekeepers have far greater trials and difficulties to meet than those of any other nation. And it is probable that many of those who may read over the methods of thrift and economy adopted by some of the best housekeepers in our land, and detailed in this work, will with a sign exclaim, that it is *impossible* for them even to attempt any such plans.... these words of comfort are offered.

Perhaps you find yourself encompassed in such sort of trials as these. Your house is inconvenient, or destitute of those facilities for doing work well which you need, and you cannot command the means to supply these deficiencies. Your domestics are so imperfectly qualified that they never can do anything *just right*, unless you stand by and attend to everything yourself, and you cannot be present in parlor, nursery, and kitchen all at once. Perhaps you are frequently left without any cook, or without a chambermaid, and sometimes without any hands but your own to do the work, and there is constant jostling and change from this cause. And perhaps you cannot get supplies, either from garden or market, such as you need, and all your calculations fail in that direction.

And perhaps your children are sickly, and rob you of rest by night, or your health is so poor that you feel no energy, or spirits to make exertions. And perhaps you never have had any training in domestic affairs, and cannot understand how to work yourself, nor how to direct others. And when you go for aid to experienced housekeepers, or cookery books, you are met by such sort of directions as these: "Take a *pinch* of this, and a *little* of that, and *considerable* of the other, and cook them till they are done *about right*." And when you cannot succeed in following such indefinite instructions, you find your neighbors and husband wondering how it is that when you have one, two, or three domestics, there should be so much difficulty about housekeeping, and such constant trouble, and miscalculation, and mistake. And then, perhaps, you lose your patience and your temper, and blame others, and others blame you, and so everything seems to be in a snarl. [p. 276-278]

To Hired Service

... consider that the great object of life to us is not *enjoyment*, but the *formation of a right character*; that such a character cannot be formed, except by *discipline*, and that the trials and difficulties of domestic life, if met in a proper spirit and manner, will, in the end, prove blessings rather than evils, by securing a measure of elevation, dignity, patience, self-control, and benevolence, that could be gained by no other methods.

[Newspaper clippings and notes inside the book for the following:}

Cure for appendicitis– taking one or two ounces of sweet oil every three hours.

A remedy for small pox –
one grain Sulphate of zinc
one grain foxglove (digittis)
half a teasponful of sugar
two tablespoons of water
When thoroughly mixed, add 4 oz. of water and take a spoonful every hour.
Also cures scarlet fever.

Cholera Preventitive
5 drops hydrocloric (sic) acid
in a cup of tea every other morning

Bloating in Cattle

spirit of ammonia in water – one tablespoon for cattle, one teaspoon for sheep. Oct. 19th, 1876.

Earliest Books in Library

Among the earliest books in Crissie's library were volumes that may have traveled West with George and Bettie:
National Class, 1830, with chapters titled "Considerations to Aid Youth in Resisting Temptation," "Necessity of Mental Exertion," "On the Evils of Lying," and one chapter "On the Characters of Adams and Jefferson."
Aunt Jane brought *The National Reader*, 1841, to the Andrews Ranch.

Children's books included *Katie Summers, A Tale for Little Readers* by Mrs. Charles Hall, London, 1875. This was a small 3"x3" book with colored pictures pasted in it. Rowland Caughlin's name was in *The House We Live In* by Vesta J. Farnsworth, 1900, a book all about the human body.

Shafer, Daniel R., A.M., *Household and Farmers' Cyclopedia or One Hundred Thousand Facts for the People*. St. Louis, Missouri and Atlanta, Georgia: Anchor Publishing Company, 1879.
"A Book for the Farmer, Mechanic, and Working Men of all Trades and Occupations, the Stock Raiser, the Household, and every Family who wants to Save Money; a Book of Solid Worth and Practical Utility, containing a Remedy for every

Ill, a Solution for every Difficulty, and a Method for every Emergency." [We need such a book today!!!]

Blake, George H., *Common-Sense Ideas for Dairymen*. Elgin, Illinois: The Elgin Dairy Report, 1900.

"Being an Exposition of the Methods Pursued by the Most Practical and Successful Dairymen in the Elgin District. Embracing Instruction in Selection, Feeding and Care of Dairy Cattle, Corn and Clover Culture, Care of Milk, Milk and Cream Testing, and Cheese and Butter Making in the Factory and on the Farm, Etc."

[Inside were several small pages of information about a bee keeping venture, and then the following recipes.]

Bleaching the hair
and used by Roman ladies
1 qt tea made from ashes of fine things
½ oz Biony [sp?]
½ celandine Roots
½ Tumeric
4 drachms Saffron
2 drachms Lilly Roots
1 drachm Flowers of Mullen
1 drachm Yellow Stickas
1 drachm Broom
1 drachm St. Johns Root
Boil those ingredients together and strain. By washing the hair frequently with this solution, it will become a beautiful flaxen color

For the Bust
½ oz Alum Water
1 oz strong chamomile (sic) water
2 oz white Brandy
apply night and morning

To keep face from becoming flabby
the white of 1 egg
one tablespoonful of honey
½ oz of Alum
Ground Barley enough to make a paste
this is beaten together and used with a mash
1 oz Spermaceti
1 oz White Wax
1 oz Olive Oil
1 Tablespoonful of Honey
melt and beat to a cream to make the face smooth and satiny

For Freckles
1 oz Sweet Almond
4 drachms Butter Almond

10 fluid oz Cherry Brandy
add
6 grains Corrosive Sublimate
6 drachms Tincture Benzoin
4 drachms Lemon Juice

For Wrinkles and preserving the skin
4 eggs (the whites of)
½ pint Rosewater
½ oz Alum
½ oil of sweet Almond
Almond meal or Oatmeal enough to form past – Beat the eggs, rosewater, alum and almond oil together and add the Almond and Oatmeal until a paste is formed thick enough to spread over mash

Aunt Martha Salve for Burns
Buy some vaseline and steep some plantain leaves in it several days on the back of the range, strain and mix in one tenth as much boracic acid and bottle it in the Vaseline jar.

Crissie's Recipe for gingerbread
1 cup molasses
1 half cup water
one large tablespoon of lard
1 teaspoonful of soda
ginger to taste
mix thick [I assume with flour] enough to roll on tins, bake in a quick oven

One book even contained a home remedy for any man who had been lynched and survived!

ENDNOTES

Chapter 1

The family name was originally Andrew, spelled without the final "s." It appears that George became the first generation named Andrews, adding the "s" after moving West.

[2] Sam P. Davis, ed., *The History of Nevada*. Las Vegas, NV: Nevada Publications, 1984. Clarks was a station on the Southern Pacific Railway, 18 miles east of Sparks. It was settled in 1862 by James Clark, who was the boss of Chinese laborers on the railroad. There is no evidence from correspondence dating back to 1862 that George ever lived at Clarks Station, and I don't know how Martha arrived at this conclusion.

[3] Myra B. Lord, "A History of the town of New London, Merrimack County, New Hampshire, 1779-1899." New London, New Hampshire. This information was sent in a 1960 letter from a relative to Crissie's daughter, Syrene, and matches a letter from the Town Clerk's office.

[4] Although there were many teachers in the Andrews family dating back to Hannah (George's mother), Martha's letters were the first written with proper punctuation, grammar, and spelling. All letters have been transcribed, and punctuation, capitalization, and spelling have been added for clarity and ease of reading. Ellipses indicate either unreadable text or deleted portions. The original letters are in The Crissie Caughlin Collection at the University of Nevada, Reno, Getchell Library, Special Collections department.

[5] This letter was unsigned but is most likely from George's father, Benjamin Andrew, based on the content.

[6] Hannah's letters seldom contained punctuation, and her handwriting was nearly illegible.

[7] The date appears to be 1861, and text of the letter refers to a February 1860 letter from George. Often letters were written with a post script or P.S. across the top and in all margins – using every possible space on the precious paper, but making it difficult to transcribe the correct date.

[8] Another unsigned letter, this one was probably written by George's sister Mary, whose letters expressed more drama and emotion than sister Martha's.

Chapter 2

[1] Stanley W. Paher, *Nevada Ghost Towns & Mining Camps*. San Diego, CA: Howell-North Books, 1970, p. 466.

[2] Bettie's youngest sister Esther married Napoleon Bonaparte Hunewill. They were also traveling to Aurora, and ultimately settled the Hunewill Ranch near Bridgeport, which still exists as a guest ranch owned by Esther Hunewill's descendants.

[3] California State Parks Web site, written by Ranger Craig Burke.

[4] Silver Mountain City is 7 miles east of Ebbetts Pass in Alpine County, California, near Markleeville. Originally called Kongsberg, the name was changed to Silver Mountain City by 1863. In 1866, the town had a population of 3,000.

[5] Thompson & West, *History of Nevada with Illustrations and Biographical Sketches of its Prominent Men & Pioneers*. Oakland, California: Thompson & West, 1881, pp. 75-78 and 624-626.

Chapter 3

[1] An excellent description of the Kennebec River settlements in the late 1700s and early 1800s is found in Laurel Thatcher Ulrich, *A Midwife's Tale: The Life of Martha Ballard, Based on Her Diary, 1785-1812.* New York: Alfred A. Knopf, 1990. Skowhegan, Maine is mentioned on page 109 in relation to a court case documented in both Martha Ballard's and Henry Sewall's diaries. Martha delivered many children in the area and tended to the sick, and although there is no mention of the Hughes family, the religious and community network, the work divided among men and women, and the community's provisions for children whose mothers died early would be similar to what Bettie Hughes experienced.

[2] See the Hunewill history by Millie Hunewill Hamblet, *The Saga of the Circle H, 1861-1961*. San Francisco, CA: The Black Vine Press, 1961. Millie was the granddaughter of Esther Hughes Hunewill, and her research helped with some information on the Hughes family.

[3] John's handwriting is difficult to decipher so his middle initial could be C., G., or B. For consistency we have chosen John C. Hughes.

[4] On this letter, the year is missing, but it was probably written in 1864 or 1865, because Bettie's son Benjamin, who was born in August 1863 was mentioned and the boom was over at Aurora.

[5] This letter may be the last one written by Harriet while Bettie and George's twins were still living.

[6] Although there is no year or envelope, this letter was probably written sometime in 1866, because Ben was born and Aunt Jane was staying with Bettie.

[7] When Harriet says here that Lizzie's loss of a son would help her understand Bettie, she is most likely referring to the deaths of Bettie's twins, Byron and Laura.

[8] A Wells, Fargo & Company's Express dated April 30, 1888 for gold valued at $200 from Mrs. Andrews is addressed to William Hughes, Redwood City.

Chapter 4

[1] Thompson & West, *History of Nevada with Illustrations and Biographical Sketches of Its Prominent Men & Pioneers*. Oakland, California: Thompson & West, 1881, p. 626.

[2]"Mrs. Caughlin Looks Into A Mirror and Recalls Some Days She Spent At Bowers'*, Nevada State Journal,* Dec. 26, 1948.

[3]Addenbrooke, Alice B. *The Mistress of the Mansion*. Palo Alto, California: Pacific Books, 1950, p. 20, 30-32.

[4]Thompson & West, p. 632.

[5]Ibid, pp. 626-628.

[6]Ibid., p. 628.

[7]The first ranch house was built on land some distance from the present location of the larger house on Mayberry Drive. That building is called the bunkhouse and now stands behind the Caughlin Ranch house at the corner of South McCarran and Mayberry. The big Caughlin Ranch house was moved from Virginia City to Reno in 1900.

[8]"Nature's Sanitarium, Reno, Nevada and Its Surroundings in the Sierras," Journal Print, Reno, Nevada. This is a small 3X5 promotional booklet that includes extensive weather information. One chapter is titled, "Whitaker Hall" by Rev. Erasmus Van Deerlin.

[9]Thompson & West, p. 641

[10]Ibid. p. 198 – 199, [drawing on page 198a]

[11]From a talk given at the annual meeting of the Historic Reno Preservation Society by Carrie Townley Porter. 2000.

[12]Doten, Alfred. *The Journals of Alfred Doten, 1849-1903*, p.1606.

[13]"Register of the Nevada State University for 1889-90," University of Nevada, Reno archives.

[14]*Artemisia, 1899*, University of Nevada yearbook, p. 19.

[15]From an undated and unnamed newspaper clipping in the Crissie Caughlin Collection.

[16]Doten, Alfred. *The Journals of Alfred Doten, 1849-1903*, pp. 1730 and 1733. Mrs. Powell was probably Jane Powell, Crissie's aunt.

Chapter 5

[1] Orvis Ring was the superintendent of public instruction for Nevada schools in 1877, according to Doten's diaries, p. ???
[2]Stanford University was built at the site of the wood mill that William Hughes operated—the same one where Bettie and George met. When it was destroyed in a spring flood, Hughes sold the property and moved to Aurora to find work.

Chapter 6

[1] *Nevada State Journal*, February 13, 1895.

[2] Laura Tucker was Crissie's bridesmaid and photographer. Her dear friend took some of the photographs found in the Crissie Caughlin collection.

[3] According to Nevada historian Elmer Rusco, Rev. Nila Maynard was a black minister, who served as the head of the Unitarian Church in Reno at the time when Ann Martin came through Nevada to get "Votes for Women." I don't know whether Crissie was involved in either Nevada's Suffrage Movement or the Unitarian Church.

[4] The Andrews ranch was 460 acres at the time of William and Crissie's marriage. James Scrugham, *History of Nevada, Vol. 2.* New York and Chicago: American Historical Society, 1935. pp. 208-210

[5] Ibid, pp. 209-210.

[6] Cornelia Caughlin died on June 12, 1886 at the age of 36 years. Reno Evening Gazette, June 13, 1886.

[7] Thomas Wren, *A History of Nevada.* New York and Chicago: The Lewis Publishing Company, 1904. pp.539-540.

[8] Mary P. Sloan diary, the Crissie Caughlin collection.

[9] *Nevada State Journal*, June 7, 1895.

[10] *Nevada State Journal,* Oct. 20, 1896.

[11] Aunt Martha caught the error in the newspaper obituary. George was born February 10, 1834, which would have made him 76 at his death, not 67.

[12] *Nevada State Journal,* Jan. 28, 1910.

[13] September 24, 1862 in San Mateo County, California.

[14] Crissie added that George had two sisters, Martha Jane and Mary Emmeline, both younger. He and Betsey had four children -- Benjamin; twins Laura and Byron, and Christina Hannah (or Harriet), "Crissie." The twins died as babies when they were about 9 months old.

[15] The Antrim Reporter, Antrim, New Hampshire, Wednesday, July 11, 1917.

[16] *Nevada State Journal*, November 15, 1897.
[17] *Nevada State Journal*, September 29, 1915.

[18] Peckham, George E., *Reminiscences of an Active Life, Nevada Historical Society Papers, Vol. II, 1917-1920.* Reno, Nevada: Nevada Historical Society, 1920, p. 134-135.

Chapter 7

[1] *Nevada State Journal*, Nov. 26, 1895 –
CAUGHLIN – In Reno, November 25, 1895, to the wife of W.H. Caughlin, a son. [Bill]

[2] *Nevada State Journal*, July 15, 1898 –
CAUGHLIN – In Reno, July 12, 1898 to the wife of W.H. Caughlin, a daughter. [Syrene]

[3] *Nevada State Journal*, March 7, 1900 –
God Giveth...
A son was born to Mr. and Mrs. W. H. Caughlin yesterday. [Rowland]

[4] *Nevada State Journal*, January 14, 1914.

[5] *Nevada State Journal*, January 15, 1914.

Chapter 8

[1] Elliott, Russell, R., *History of Nevada*. Lincoln, Nebraska, University of Nebraska Press, 1973, p. 173.

[2] Crissie's Legal Documents, Special Collections, University of Nevada, Reno.
[3] Thomas Wren, *A History of Nevada.* New York and Chicago: The Lewis Publishing Company, 1904. pp. 539-540

[4] Joe Rondo, Nevada State Prison file NSP 2036, Nevada State Library and Archives.

[5] Oral history interview with Alma Westegard and Shiela Lonie, by Victoria Ford, Aug. 11, 2000.

[6] Crissie was very suspicious of the Japanese during the war years.

[7] Min was Minerva Hughes Collin, Crissie's cousin and dear friend. At this point, Crissie's cousin Minerva Collins is married to her stepson, Ed Caughlin. They were all dear friends for life.

Chapter 9

[1] Bremer, Lynn, "Featured Historic Nevada Woman: Mary Stoddard Doten," *Nevada Women's History Project News*, Vol. 7, No. 3, August 2002, pp. 8-9.
[2] *The Journals of Alfred Doten,* 1849-1903, p. 1606, p.1733, p. 2020

[3] Biographical sketches compiled from "Emma Nevada, at 4, on the road to singing stardom," by Phillip I. Earl, *Reno Gazette-Journal,* April 24, 1988, p. 2e. and "Emma Nevada, An American Diva," by Eugene F. Gray, 1999 at *www.msu.edu/~graye/emma*

4 "Reflections, Reminders of our past taken from the pages of the *San Francisco Examiner*," January 1900-December 1999, p. W4.

5 Land & Land, *A Short History of Reno*. Reno, University of Nevada Press, 1995. p. 36.

6 "Sports Stories of the 20th Century in Northern Nevada," *Reno Gazette-Journal*, Dec. 12, 1999, pp. 1D and 8D.

7 Ibid., p. 8D

8 Land & land, *A Short History of Reno*. Reno, University of Nevada Press, 1995. p. 36.

9 Phillip I. Earl, "This Was Nevada: Program to Mark 75th Anniversary of Johnson-Jeffries Fight" *Prospector Weekly News*, Vol. 8, No. 3, June 19, 1985.

10 Amaral, Anthony, *Will James: The Last Cowboy Legend*. Reno: Unive sity of Nevada Press, 1980. pp. 57-62.

11 Frederick Turner, "The Artist whose cowboys are based mostly on himself," *Smithsonian*, February 1988, p. 172.

12 [Unidentified newspaper article among Crissie's files dated January 14, 1941, with obituary of Lorenzo Latimer.]

Chapter 10

1 Thompson & West, *History of Nevada with Illustrations and Biographical Sketches of its Prominent Men & Pioneers*. Oakland, California: Thompson & West, 1881, p. 634.

2 Crissie Caughlin Collection, Getchell Library Special Collections Department.

3 January 1935, Reno Evening Gazette.

4 Among letters my grandmother wrote to her daughters Syrene and Betsy during the three-year court case was a slip of paper that said, "Let every man be occupied in the highest way of which his nature is capable; and die with the consciousness that he has done his best."

Chapter 11

1 Unknown and undated newspaper clipping.

Chapter 12

1 Unknown newspaper clipping dated Aug. 3, 1955.

Crissie Caughlin Bibliography

Addenbrooke, Alice B. *The Mistress of the Mansion*. Palo Alto, California: Pacific Books, 1950.

Amaral, Anthony, *Will James: The Last Cowboy Legend*. Reno: University of Nevada Press, 1980.

Artemisia, 1899, University of Nevada yearbook.

Bremer, Lynn, "Featured Historic Nevada Woman: Mary Stoddard Doten," *Nevada Women's History Project News*, Vol. 7, No. 3, August 2002.

California State Parks Web site, written by Ranger Craig Burke, 2002.

Crissie Caughlin Collection, Special Collections, Getchell Library, University of Nevada, Reno.

Davis, Sam P., ed., *The History of Nevada*. Las Vegas, NV: Nevada Publications, 1984.

Doten, Alfred. *The Journals of Alfred Doten, 1849-1903*.

Doten, Alfred. *The Journals of Alfred Doten, 1849-1903*.

Earl, Phillip I., "Emma Nevada, at 4, on the Road to Singing Stardom," *Reno Gazette-Journal,* April 24, 1988.

Earl, Phillip I., "This Was Nevada: Program to Mark 75th Anniversary of Johnson-Jeffries Fight," *Prospector Weekly News*, Vol. 8, No. 3, June 19, 1985.

Elliott, Russell, R., *History of Nevada*. Lincoln, Nebraska: University of Nebraska Press 1973.

Gray, Eugene F., "Emma Nevada, An American Diva," at *www.msu.edu/~graye/emma*, 1999.

Hamblet, Millie Hunewill, *The Saga of the Circle H, 1861-1961*. San Francisco, CA: The Black Vine Press, 1961.

Joe Rondo, Nevada State Prison file NSP 2036, Nevada State Library and Archives.

Land & Land, *A Short History of Reno*. Reno, Nevada: University of Nevada Press, 1995. p. 36.

Laxalt, Robert. *Nevada: A History*. New York: W. W. Norton, 1977; and Reno: University of Nevada Press.

Lord, Myra B., "A History of the Town of New London, Merrimack County, New

Hampshire, 1779-1899." New London, New Hampshire.

Nature's Sanitarium, Reno, Nevada and Its Surroundings in the Sierras," Journal Print, Reno, Nevada. "Whitaker Hall" by Rev. Erasmus Van Deerlin.
Nevada State Journal, February 13, 1895 - January 15, 1914.

"Mrs. Caughlin Looks Into A Mirror and Recalls Some Days She Spent At Bowers'," *Nevada State Journal*, Dec. 26, 1948.

Oral history interview with Alma Westegard and Shiela Lonie, by Victoria Ford, Aug. 11, 2000.

Paher, Stanley W., *Nevada Ghost Towns & Mining Camps*. San Diego, CA: Howell-North Books, 1970, p. 466.

Porter, Carrie Townley, presentation to the annual meeting of the Historic Reno Preservation Society, 2000.

Rusco, Elmer, conversation re: Rev. Maynard, Unitarian Church in Reno, 2000.

Peckham, George E., "Reminiscences of an Active Life," *Nevada Historical Society Papers, Vol. II, 1917-1920*. Reno, Nevada: Nevada Historical Society, 1920.

"Register of the Nevada State University for 1889-90," University of Nevada, Reno Archives.
Reno Evening Gazette, June 13, 1886, January 1935.

"Sports Stories of the 20th Century in Northern Nevada," *Reno Gazette-Journal*, Dec. 12, 1999.

"Reflections, Reminders of Our Past taken from the pages of the San Francisco Examiner," *San Francisco Examiner*. January 1900-December 1999.

Scrugham, James Graves, *A History of Nevada, Vol. 2*. Chicago & New York: The American Historical Society, Inc. 1935.

The Antrim Reporter, Antrim, New Hampshire, Wednesday, July 11, 1917.

Thompson & West, *History of Nevada with Illustrations and Biographical Sketches of Its Prominent Men & Pioneers*. Oakland, California: Thompson & West, 1881.

Turner, Frederick, "The Artist whose cowboys are based mostly on himself," *Smithsonian*, February 1988, p. 172.

Ulrich, Laurel Thatcher, *A Midwife's Tale: The Life of Martha Ballard. Based on Her Diary, 1785-1812*. New Yourk: Alfred A. Knopf, 1990.

Wren, Thomas, *A History of Nevada*. New York & Chicago: The Lewis Publishing Company, 1904.

Index

Almanac, 26

Alum Creek, 143, 166, 175, 209

Andrew, Benjamin Randall, 15-18, 102, 106, 201, 209

Andrew, Hannah Buchanan, 9, 15-19, 21-22, 102, 106, 201, 209

Andrew, Martha Jane (Byers), 16-18, 22-27, 46, 49, 68-70, 102, 104-106, 128-129, 168, 200-202, 204, 209

Andrew, Mary Emeline French (Cochrane), 16-18, 21-23, 26, 45, 104, 106, 201, 204

Andrew, Samuel, 16, 20, 209

Andrew, Sarah Peaslee, 16

Andrews, Bettie Hughes, 9, 13, 15, 18, 27, 29, 30-35, 37-38, 39-49, 51-53, 55-57, 59-64, 67-68, 70, 74, 76, 81, 84, 86, 88-90, 93, 99, 102, 106, 116, 121, 135, 137, 155, 186, 198, 201-204, 209, 212

Andrews, Benjamin Howard, 19, 35, 37, 39, 41, 43-44, 46, 59, 61, 63-64, 66-67, 70-71, 75, 79, 80, 81-83, 84-85, 86, 90, 91, 96, 139, 155, 157, 202, 204, 209

Andrews, Byron (cousin), 22

Andrews, Byron (twin son of George and Bettie), 35, 39, 41, 44, 46, 48, 59, 202, 204

Andrews, Crissie Harriet, Is found throughout the book

Andrews, George Washington, 13, 15, 16-25, 26-27, 29-32, 34-41, 43-49, 53, 56-59, 61, 63-65, 67-70, 84-90, 93, 99-100, 102, 104, 116, 128, 135, 139, 142, 155, 161, 166-68, 170, 173-74, 177, 181, 187, 195, 198-99, 201-204, 208-209

Andrews, Laura (twin daughter of George and Bettie), 29, 33-35, 37, 39-41, 44, 47-48, 51, 59, 194, 204

Andrews Ranch, 68- 70, 90, 93, 96, 102, 115, 135, 137-138, 198, 204

Amaral, Anthony, 160

Argentine District, 36

Aurora, 29-31, 34-35, 45, 53-54, 57-63, 102, 107, 112, 130, 201-203

Austin District, 94

Australia, 93-95, 107-108, 143

Baer, Max, 159

Baptist, 91

Baroli, A., 170

Belton, John, 173

Belton, Marion, 173

Berrum, L. W. 168

Betsy Caughlin Donnelly Park, 179

Bowers, Eilley Orrum, 67-68, 185

Bowers' Mansion, 67, 152, 157, 183, 185

Bowers, Persia, 67, 157, 185

Bowers, Sandy, 13, 67-68
Briggs, Rhoda, 51, 107
Brooklins, C.J. (store), 77
Brown, George H., 77-78
Buscaglia, D. 169-170
Burton, George, 101
Byers, Rev. Joseph H., 74, 106
Byers, Winifred, 106

California
    Angel's Camp, 35
    Bridgeport, 53, 55, 57, 61, 64, 74, 76, 106, 113, 145, 201
    Bodie, 52, 64, 74-76, 107-108
    Calavaras County, 35
    Oakland, 56, 107-108, 178, 191
    Eureka, 83
    Half Moon Bay, 33, 102
    Mayfield, 127
    Monterey, 146
    Murphy's, 35
    Nevada City, 53, 156
    Pescadero, 29, 32-34
    Sacramento, 11, 108-109, 127, 129
    San Francisco, 18, 34-35, 45-46, 52-53, 56, 62, 78, 94, 102, 106, 112-113, 126-127, 131, 144, 146, 157, 164, 176, 182, 187, 195, 202, 206-208, 210, 216, 221
    San Mateo, 35, 57, 85-86, 90, 204
    Searsville, 30, 47, 57, 59-62, 64-65, 84-85, 99
    Silver Mountain City, 35, 45-46, 48, 102, 202
    Stockton, 35
    Woodside, 35, 40, 53, 90

Callahan, Chick, 143, 173
Callahan, Joe, 153
Camp Reno, 73
Capurro, B. & Sons, 166, 169, 170, 210
Capurro, Ben, 168
Capurro, Ernest, 124
Capurro, Gus, 124
Capurro, John, 168
Capurro, Mina, 124
Carmelite nuns, 15, 173
Carter, Bob, 129
Catholic, 33, 96, 115
Caughlin, Elizabeth "Betsy" Norene (Donnelly), 105, 108, 116, 123-124, 129, 174
Caughlin, Albert, 94, 97, 99, 108, 129

Caughlin, Arthur, 94, 97, 98, 108, 129-130
Caughlin, Edward, 94, 99, 108, 129, 205
Caughlin, Jack (brother), 93, 107-109
Caughlin, Jerry, 107-109, 126
Caughlin, John (son), 97
Caughlin, John H. (father), 94
Caughlin, Honora, 94
Caughlin Ranch, 9, 11, 15, 89, 90, 101, 134-137, 139-140, 143, 155, 157, 159-161, 166, 172-176, 180, 203
Caughlin, Rowland A., 116, 121-122, 124, 126, 128-129, 145-146, 149, 177, 198, 205
Caughlin, Syrene Pearl, 68, 105, 115-116, 120-122, 124-126, 129-131, 134, 138-139, 145-149, 151, 162, 173-174, 178, 183-185, 187, 190, 205-206
Caughlin, William Hughes "Bill", 115-116, 124-125, 129, 143, 156, 174
Caughlin, William Henry (sheriff), 89, 93-102, 108, 115, 125-126, 129-130, 137, 139-143, 145, 149, 156-157, 174
Central Pacific Railroad, 68, 89, 135
Century Club, 111, 148, 155, 184
Chism's Creamery, 141
Christian, 22, 27, 71, 105
Circle H Ranch, 106
Civil War, 13, 15, 22-24, 52-53, 60
Clark, Pick, 52, 58
Clark's Station, Nevada, 16, 201
Clemens, Sam, 31
Clough, Hugh, 23
Clough, Joseph, 23, 25
Clow, Barney, 168
Commercial Row, 151
Collins, Dr. Asa Weston, 127, 131
Comstock Lode, 36-37, 67-68, 155
Corvallis, Oregon, 99, 102-104
Crescent Creamery, 141
Crisles, Clara, 157, 185
Crissie Caughlin Park, 15, 176
Curler, Judge B.F., 170
Curly, 149
Daugherty, W.B., 76, 79
Davidson, Mrs. John, 157, 181, 185
Democrat, 26, 145
Dixon, John, 112
Donnelly, Roger, 133-134, 177
Donner Lake, 72, 124-125, 130
Doten, Alfred, 77, 80, 83, 155, 203, 205, 207
Doten, Mary Stoddard, 77, 155-156, 205, 207
Doten, Milly, 155
Eason, Bob, 126

Eastern Star, 181, 187
Eaton, Alfred, 23
Eaton, Charlie, 81-82
Eaton, John, 23
Eichelburg, Bessie, 12
Elko, Nevada, 27, 68-70, 156
England, Liverpool, 157
Episcopal, 71, 91
Everett, John, 103-104
Farmers' Bank, 145
Federal Land Bank, 169
Fordham, Prilla, 11, 149
Francis, Grace, 191
Francis, John Hunter, 191
Francis, Steven Tyler, 191
Francis, Syrene Scharbach, 191
Frederick, Marcus, 81
French family, 16-17, 25, 102
French, Greene, 17
French, Molly Page, 16, 102
Frey, Joseph, 135, 168, 170
Ferris Ranch, 110, 141, 173, 185-186
Galena Creek Ditch Company, 166
Galena District, 36
Garden Gate Club, 181-182, 184, 187
Geiger, George, 100
Glendale Irrigation Ditch Company, 166
Gould & Curry mine, 37, 48
Groesbeck, Dora, 161, 163-164
Grove, Ned, 145
Grove, Rose, 145
Griswold, Grace, 83
Guild, Judge Clark, 170
Hanson, Peter, 168
Hatch, A.J., 102
Hearne, Johnny, 75, 107
Hearne, Moses, 52, 107
Himmelberger, Jake, 146-147
Holcomb, Grove, 168
Homemakers Club, 151, 181-182, 184
Hughes, Esther, 45, 51-56, 59-60, 62-64, 75-76, 85, 106-107, 137-138, 145, 201-202
Hughes, Hannah (Stella) (Hearne), 51-52, 61, 64, 75-76, 107
Hughes, Harriet, 29, 35, 41, 52-53, 56-57, 59-60, 63, 65-66, 78, 84, 86, 99, 106-107, 202, 204
Hughes, Jane, 27, 45, 51-53, 56, 59-63, 66, 69, 74-76, 107, 137, 198, 202-203
Hughes, Minerva "Minnie", 65-66, 70, 126, 131, 146, 152-153, 205

Hughes, Rachel, 45, 49, 51, 53, 60, 62-63, 75
Hughes, Syrene, 45, 51-52, 58-60, 107-108
Hughes, William, 18, 29, 30, 34, 41, 51-54, 56-63, 65, 84, 106-108, 118, 174, 202-203,
Humphrey Supply Company, 166
Huniwell, Napoleon Bonaparte, 52-53, 55, 60, 63, 201
Huniwell, Frank, 61, 64-65
Huniwell, Alice Hyde, 53, 75, 131, 144
Huniwell, Lucile, 53, 74, 107, 138
Huniwell, Millie, 53, 57, 74, 77, 106, 107, 130, 138, 202, 207
Huniwell, Stanley, 53, 74, 130, 137-138, 144
Hunter Creek, 152
Hurst, Sadie, 112
Hymers, Nell, 112
Isthmus of Panama, 18, 53, 102, 105
James, Alice, 160-161
James, Will, 160-161
Jap Flats, 161, 171, 173
Jeffries, Jim, 157, 159, 206-207
Johnson, Jack, 157-159, 206-207
Kearney, William "Bill" M., 166, 168, 170, 171-172
Kentucky, Crab Orchard, 26, 106
Kietzke, A., 166
Lake Ditch, 151, 167-170, 173
Lake Tahoe, 11, 53, 147, 164
Landis, Martha W., 168
Last Chance Ditch, 89, 103, 135, 149, 152, 165-170, 173
Latimer Club, 164, 182
Latimer, Lorenzo P., 125, 161, 162-164
Laughton, George, 81, 129
Laughton School, 124
Layton, Mrs. B.F., 91
Laxalt, Robert, 157, 207
Lee, Stacie Scharbach Williamson, 7, 184, 191
Lincoln, Abraham, 23, 24
Lincoln Hall, University of Nevada, 79
London, Jack, 157
Lonie, Donald, 174-176
Mackay, Mrs. John, 183
Maine, 15, 29, 45, 51-53, 60, 63, 102, 143, 202
Malone, George W., 168
Marchessi, Madame, 156
Martin, H.R., 151, 168
Masonic, 91, 129
Masons, 37, 91
Mayberry, James, 165, 168, 170

Mayberry Drive/Street, 13, 15, 89, 135, 139-140, 157, 165-166, 174, 176, 186-187, 203
Maynard, Reverend, 93, 204, 208
McCutchins' Guards, 23
McCarran Boulevard, 15, 68, 139, 161, 167, 173, 175-176, 203
McCarran, P.A., 166
McKinley School, 119
McKissick's Opera House, 80
Mexico, 146, 182
Mikkelson, Steve, 177
Mikkelson, Kris, 178
Mill Street, Reno, 95, 99, 115, 137, 163
Minden Bank, 144, 145
Misser, Austin, 24
Montreux Golf Course, 176
Moore, Howard "Dinty", 99, 133, 134
Moore, Lucinda D., 99
Morrill, Enoch, 168
Morrill Hall, University of Nevada, 74-75, 79
Mount Davidson, Nevada, 36
Napa College, California, 80, 82-83, 90
Nay, Winslow, 168, 170
Nevada Building and Supply Company, 131
Nevada, Emma Wixom, 156-157, 205, 207

Nevada,
  Austin, 108, 156
  Carson City, 11, 38, 108, 157, 165-167, 185
  Dayton, 38
  Fallon, 147
  Fernley, 147
  Franktown, 36-37, 49, 67, 161
  Gardnerville, 53, 144
  Genoa, 38, 53
  Gold Hill, 36-38, 155
  Lyon County, 130, 144
  Ophir, 36, 37, 44, 67
  Ragtown, 35
  Reno, 9, 11, 13, 15, 27, 35, 42, 49, 68, 70-72, 74, 75, 77-81, 84-86, 88, 90-91, 93-94, 96, 99-100, 102-105, 108-109, 111, 115, 125, 127, 129, 131, 139, 141, 146, 150-151, 153, 155, 157, 159-168, 170, 173-177, 180, 182-183, 185-187, 190, 201, 203-208, 214
  Smith Valley, 130, 144
  Steamboat Creek, 35
  Verdi, 93
  Verdi Road, 13, 101, 109, 135, 139-140, 148, 157, 159, 170, 173, 187

Verdi Lumber Company, 166
Virginia City, 35-38, 42, 44-45, 48, 53, 67-68, 77, 94, 102, 138-139, 155-157, 174, 177, 183, 203
Wadsworth, 77, 78, 166
Washoe City, 13, 36-42, 44, 46-48, 53, 60, 63, 67-68, 102, 155, 187
Washoe Lake, 36, 40, 141, 166
Washoe Valley, 35-36, 48, 67-68, 135, 161
Wassau Valley, 35-36
Yerington, 130

Nevada State Prison, 146, 205, 207
Nevada State University/University of Nevada, 11, 74-75, 79-85, 130, 131, 149, 187, 201, 203
Nevada Theater, 80

New Hampshire, 15-16, 27, 29, 38, 45, 68-70, 143, 173, 177
    Andover, 105
    Antrim, 18, 68, 102, 105-106, 128, 204, 208
    Concord, 23-24
    New London, 16-18, 20-26, 102, 105-106, 201, 207-208
    North Sutton, 17, 105
    Orange, 17
    Sutton, 16, 23

New London Academy, 106
New York, 18, 29, 134, 149, 155
Nixon Avenue, 149
Old Long, 41, 43
Oregon, 93, 99, 103, 176
Orr Water Ditch Company, 166
Palo Alto Ranch, 185
Peavine Peak, 141
Peckham, George, 166, 204, 208
Peers, Alex, 65
Peers, Lizzie, 59, 61-62, 65, 202
Piedmont Lumber Company, 178-179
Pierce, Minerva, 164, 182
Piretto, V., 169-170
Platt, Samuel, 166
Plumb, Duey, 129
Plumb Lane, 68, 135, 161, 167, 173, 181
Pope, Rev. W.B., 91
Porter, Reuben, 23, 25
Porter, Jerome, 25
Powers (store in Silver Mountain City), 41, 43
Prohibition laws, 74

Public Service Commission, 165, 167, 169, 170
Que, 148
Raggio, B., 166
Realization Company, 168
Reed, Ruth, 100
Redwoods in California, 18, 39
Reno Development Company, 166
Reno Golf Club, 168
Reno Power Light and Water Company, 166
Reno Wheelmen, 108
Republican, 23, 26, 94
Riley, Mrs. Nevada Wilson, 164
Ring, Orvis, 49, 81, 83, 203
Riverside Mill Company, 166
Robert Steele Corporation, 166
Rowe, Wingate, 23
Russell, Oliver, 23
Ryder, Linnie, 108
Sargent, Jack, 23-24
Seagrave, Asa Weston, 182, 190
Seagrave, Edward, 131, 150
Seagrave, Shiela Marion, 131, 190
Semenza, A., 166
Sessions, J.O., 166
Scharbach, Bob, 81, 183
Scharbach, Richard, 176-177
Scharbach, Stacie, 184, 191
Scharbach, Syrene, 190
Scheeline Banking and Trust Company, 166
Schiappacasse, Alma, 11, 149-150, 169-170
Schiappacasse, John, 130
Schiappacasse, Laura, 130
Schiappacasse, Mike, 130
Schmitt, Leo F., 169
Scolari, Lizzie, 152
Scott Ranch Ditch Company, 166
Sharon, Will, 153
Shaughnessy, J.F., 168
Shaver, J.W., 168
Sierra Nevada College, 176
Sierra Street, Reno, 70, 85
Sill, Kate, 71
Silver Peak, 46
Skyline Boulevard, 15, 173-174
Sloan, Cornelia J., 94, 96-98, 204
Sloan, Mary P., 96

Smith Valley, 130, 144
Sontag, John, 101
Spanish Springs Valley Ditch Company, 166
Spencer, Rev. G.M., 77
Stanford University, 71, 85, 203
Star Barrel House saloon, 146
Steamboat Ditch, 149, 167, 173-174
Stewart Hall, University of Nevada, 79
Stinson, Ed, 25
Stoddard, Millie, 77
Stoddard, Sarah, 155
Suzie, 88-90
Talbot decree, 168
Territorial legislature, 36
Territory of Nevada, 36
Thompson, W.R., 171
Thyes and Reese Crystal Saloon, 70, 85
Truckee Meadows, 77, 102, 116, 135, 165, 167, 170
Truckee River, 15, 68, 89, 90, 101-103, 112, 122, 126, 137, 140, 143, 162, 167-168, 173, 175-176
Truckee River General Electric Company, 166
Tucker, Laura, 96, 110, 159
Twain, Mark, 31, 148
Union, 23-25
United Nevada Bank, 165, 168-169
U.S.S. Huntington, 129-130
Verdi Lumber Company, 166
Veterans Hospital, 130
Virginia-Carson Railroad, 68
Virginia Street, Reno, 70, 99
Wadsworth Light and Power Company, 166
Walker River, 53, 113
Washoe County Bank, 151, 166
Washoe County, 36-37, 68, 86, 93-94, 99, 102, 107, 129, 135, 151, 176, 179, 187
Washoe County Sheriff, 89, 174
Washoe Zephyrs, 141
W.C.T.U. (Women's Christian Temperance Union), 106
Wells Estate Company, 166
Wells Fargo, 40-42, 101, 104, 139, 202
Wheeler, D.C., 135, 165-166, 168
Whitaker, Bishop Ozzie William, 71
Whitaker Park, 74
White Pine, 94, 108
Williamson, Robert, 191
Williamson, Whitney, 11, 191
Wilson, Wayne T., 167

Wixom, Dr. William, 108, 156
Wixom, Kate Caughlin, 156
Woman's Missionary Alliance, 106
Woman's Relief Corps, 106
Woodburn, Thatcher & Thompson, 171
Yager, M.L., 168

The Author

SHIELA LONIE was born in San Francisco and grew up in Berkeley. She graduated from the Anna Head School for Girls in 1943. At an early age, she studied voice from William Chamberlain in Berkeley, Professor Horacio T. Cogswell at the University of California and with Enid Ottero in New York. After the death of her father, she returned to Berkeley and joined a group of old friends who were starting the "Straw Hat Review" in the old Lafayette Town Hall.

Three years later she met and married Dr. Robert Scharbach and they had three children. Four years after Dr. Scharbach's death, Shiela met and married Don Lonie, a developer from Portland, Oregon. They traveled around the world and finally ended up living at Incline Village, Nevada. During those years, she turned to another of her dreams and started painting. She studied with Catherine Hagen, who taught color painting classes in Berkeley, and many other teachers around the Bay Area. Later, while living at Indian Wells, California, she began teaching her color classes to other aspiring artists.

Today, she lives in Reno and teaches color classes at her home studio. From early childhood, she spent summers at her grandmother's, the Caughlin Ranch in Reno. Since her grandmother and mother were both born in Nevada, she feels as though she has returned home.

Colophon

Designed and produced by Bob Blesse at the Black Rock Press,
University of Nevada, Reno. The typeface is Meridien,
designed by Adrian Frutiger in 1954. The layout
and design were done in Adobe InDesign. Thanks to
April Grenot and Katherine Clark for their assistance, and
to Vicki Davies and Jacque Sunstrand for their patience.
Printed at Sheridan Books, Ann Arbor, Michigan.